The Birth of the Despot

THE BIRTH
OF THE DESPOT

*Venice and
the Sublime Porte*

Lucette Valensi

Translated by Arthur Denner

Cornell University Press
ITHACA AND LONDON

Originally published in French under the title
Venise et la Sublime Porte: La naissance du despote,
© 1987 by Hachette.

The publisher gratefully acknowledges the assistance
of the French Ministry of Culture in defraying part of
the cost of the translation.

Translation copyright © 1993 by Cornell University

First published 1993 by Cornell University Press
First printing, Cornell Paperbacks, 2009

International Standard Book Number 0-8014-2480-1 (cloth)
Library of Congress Catalog Card Number 93-1352

Printed in the United States of America

*Librarians: Library of Congress cataloging information appears on the
last page of the book.*

⊗ The paper in this book meets the minimum requirements of the
American National Standard for Information Sciences–Permanence of
Paper for Printed Library Materials, ANSI Z39.48-1984.

Contents

The Birth of the Despot

Overture

The present king of this great empire, who came to power at the tender age of fourteen with the deposal of his uncle Mustafa, was so well thought of that each and every heart was filled with great hope for his success. It was universally believed that once the wrongs committed by his brother Osman had been redressed, he would become the best prince the house of Ottoman had ever had. But in the space of only a few years, he demonstrated just how far human judgment can err in predicting the future. For just as the radiance of a beautiful morning does not ensure that the day will be clear, because often the opposite occurs; or as it is with the calm of the sea: the more peaceful it is at the outset of a voyage, the greater the risk and more manifest the danger should violent and impetuous winds come to trouble it; so it was with this prince, who proved totally different from expectations. After allowing himself for a time to be governed by his mother and his ministers, and after enduring, out of fear and with great bitterness, abuses against him by the military, who demanded the heads of his principal ministers and his greatest favorites in the seraglio (and not satisfied with that, murdered his brother-in-law, the grand vizier Cafis, so near him that his clothes were splattered with blood as he looked on with such great horror and fear that for two days he remained stupefied and beside himself); then, having been comforted by Bostangi Bassi, who was Achmet Bassà, and by Cussein Effendi Mufti, who together roused him to courage and retribution—and who soon thereafter were strangled on his orders—he turned all his thoughts to revenge, so completely that, overcome by its seductions, stirred by indignation, and moved by anger, he proved unrivaled in savagery and cruelty. On those days that he did not take a human life, he did not feel that he was happy and gave no sign of gladness. But when many were brought before him to be executed, which was more often the case, he was joyous and cheerful for all to see, and therefore those who knew him would await such circumstances to ask of him some favor or reward. And when his ministers wished to ingratiate themselves with him, they would present him with heads if they could not offer gold or silver. When he was away from the city, arrangements were made for those in charge of the government to round up all persons who had been sentenced to death, so that their great number might bring consolation to his soul and augment his good will. And it was a matter of great importance that for his most splendid and pomp-filled entrances, he wanted his route lined with decapitated bodies. Whereas other princes on such occasions grant pardons, liberate prisoners, and commute sentences to win their people's love and affection, this one wanted to see streets coated with blood rather than strewn with roses, to have his severity appear in all its rigor lest, through some act of generosity, there be seen in him the glimmerings of mercy.[1]

Thus did Venetian ambassador Pietro Foscarini in 1637 describe the Ottoman emperor Murad IV, whose regime he characterized as "the most immoderate, the most extravagant . . . a power absolute and *despotic*."[2]

Words have their histories. They emerge, drift about, shape our perceptions and our ways of thinking, fix themselves in the map of our ideas, before being submerged by new concepts. The words *despote, despotique,* and *despotisme* appeared in a French dictionary for the first time in 1720. The concept of despotism seems to have been formed at the end of the seventeenth century, and before long the term described a political system in which the absolute power of a monarch went hand in hand with social servitude. Montesquieu, with *L'esprit des lois* (1748), made the concept of despotism a permanent fixture in European political thought: he disassembled the mechanism, observed the connections between the parts, and assigned it a place in political taxonomy by contrasting it to democratic, aristocratic, and monarchical forms of governments. But the word "despotism" continued its career and, gathering adjectives here and there, yielded new varieties.[3] Montesquieu had advanced the idea of a stable relationship between natural conditions—the climates—and political systems. After him, the physiocrats introduced the notion of legal despotism, a variety they believed native to China. For François Quesnay, a staunch opponent of Montesquieu's theses, ancient wisdom and natural law were the basis of the emperor of China's authority.[4] In Western climates, despotism somehow brightened, became "enlightened despotism," a notion that came after the fact and had more success with historians than with political philosophers. Frederick the Great of Prussia, Leopold II of Tuscany, Catherine the Great of Russia, Maria Theresa and Joseph II of Austria all belonged to the family of eighteenth-century enlightened despots.[5] But in Asia it was a different variety of despotism that flourished. In "those sad regions" Nicolas-Antoine Boulanger saw

the man who has no will kissing his chains, the man with no property or safe fortune worshiping his tyrant, the man with no knowledge of man or reason and whose only virtue is fear; and what is truly surprising and puzzling is that it is there that men take their servitude to heroic extremes, numb themselves to their own existence and with pious imbecility bless the savage whim that often takes their lives, the only thing they might be said to possess but which, according to the law of their prince, belongs to him alone to do with as he pleases.[6]

Which Orient was this, which Asia? For Boulanger, it was all Asia, ancient and modern, "plunged in every age in sloth and servitude," while "history shows us Europe ever brave, ever jealous of her freedom."[7] Abraham Anquetil-Duperron's denials notwithstanding, despotism continued its oriental career in various avatars.[8] We will not follow that career but rather will make our way upstream through history. If Pietro Foscarini speaks of despotic government a good century before *L'esprit des lois*, when did the character of the despot first appear? What role did the Sublime Porte—which, we must not forget, was in Europe—play in the sixteenth- and seventeenth-century European imagination? How was the Ottoman system perceived and how was it described?

We will question experts: Pietro Foscarini was one of them, having spent three years in Istanbul. Before him and after him came other ambassadors from the Venetian republic who had also resided in the imperial capital. Since the thirteenth century, Venice had maintained a permanent representative in Constantinople who bore the title of *bailo* and was responsible for defending the persons and property of his fellow citizens. Even after the capture of Constantinople by the Turks in 1453, those orders stood and the post remained occupied without interruption—except in times of war between Venice and the Porte—until the end of the Republic.[9] In theory, the ambassador would spend two years at his post, longer when there was a delay in his successor's arrival. And when the *bailo* returned to Venice, he was expected, like every ambassador Venice had stationed in the great capitals, to present before a public session of the Senate and in the presence of the doge, a detailed report concerning the state he had just left.

With remarkable consistency, Venice kept current a precise inventory of the forces, resources, and potential weaknesses of all the kingdoms and principalities that counted at the time and on that information based its political and military strategy. At the same time, as one of these ambassadors who had returned from Istanbul noted in 1612, the Republic had "before its eyes, as in a theater, a representation of the world, nature, and the laws and styles of the various peoples."[10] Supplementing the ambassadorial reports on the Ottoman Empire were those prepared by the Republic's orators, envoys extraordinary who would come to Istanbul to conclude a treaty, to congratulate the sultan on his accession or on a military victory, or perhaps to attend the festivities for the circumcision of a prince. Not all these reports have been preserved and recovered—and those ambassadors who died at their posts did not leave any—but between the beginning of the sixteenth century and Foscarini's return, more than forty envoys from the Republic came before the Senate to give their accounts of what they had seen.

It is this performance before the Venetian assembly that the reader is now invited to attend.

PART ONE

Judith

The Venetian ambassadors belonged to the Republic's patriciate and thus stood at an intersection of three spaces, those of empirical observation, political action, and humanism. They were men in the field, observers whose residency in the Ottoman Empire allowed them to study its machinery at their leisure. They were men of action, with the mission of following in minute detail the operations of the center of the system, and they directly influenced the strategy of the Republic. They were sons of the most highly educated elite and were steeped in humanist culture.

Preferably, they would be selected from among citizens who had frequented the schools of Padua and, later, those of the Rialto and Venice's erudite circles.[11] The University of Padua, during the Renaissance, was one of the major European centers in the revival of classical studies. And in the education of the Venetian elite, politics, the civil science, lay at the heart of those studies. Greek had been taught at Padua since 1463, and in 1497 a course was instituted which had Aristotle as its basic Greek text, stripped of centuries of scholastic commentary. The Venetians thus had direct access to classical political thought. In 1546, during his Venetian exile, Florentine Antonio Brucioli produced the first Italian translation of Aristotle's *Politics*, and a few years later, in a telling indication of the particular attention that Venetian culture paid to politics in various forms, a senatorial decree made this work required reading in the Paduan schools.[12]

Once they had completed their studies, the young patricians

took their expected places within the humanist circles. They became patrons of the arts and were sometimes creators themselves, as artists or intellectuals. The dreams and values of some of them we know, as they gave them form in stone and in books. Marcantonio Barbaro, ambassador to the Porte in 1573, had trained in Padua and earned his doctorate there. He came from a family of patrician patrons and continued the tradition with his brother Daniele, archbishop of Aquileia. Daniele Barbaro, who had traveled to Rome in the company of Palladio, published an annotated edition of Vitruvius in 1556. Soon afterward, the two brothers commissioned the Maser villa, one of sixteenth-century Italy's loveliest. The plans were the work of Palladio; the frescoes are Veronese's. The villa realized in all its splendor the great humanist architect's conception of order, which held that "beauty will result from the form and correspondence of the whole with respect to the parts, of the parts with regard to each other, and of these again to the whole; that the structure may appear an entire and compleat body, wherein each member agrees with the other, and all necessary to compose what you intend to form."[13] The villa also embodied the ideal of the great agricultural estate as country retreat where the landowner could oversee its operations while devoting himself to reading and reflection, in imitation of the sages of antiquity, who, again in Palladio's words, "would retire to such places." Marcantonio himself apparently had a hand in building the nymphaeum, and several of its statues have been attributed to him as well. Elected to the Senate in 1577, he participated in choosing the plans for the Church of the Redeemer: it is circular in layout, in the manner of the votive temples of antiquity and because the circle was thought to be the figure most befitting the dignity of the Republic. Marcantonio Barbaro was also partly responsible for the construction of the Procuratie Nuove at the Piazza San Marco.[14] His ambassadorial report on the Ottoman Empire was one of the most widely read in Europe in the sixteenth century.

Leonardo Donà, ambassador to the Porte in 1595 and doge in

1606, had been educated by the preceptors at the academies, then by those at the universities of Padua and Bologna. In the seventeenth century, the political and intellectual elites were still one and the same. Giovanni Capello was a philosopher and a mathematician. Giambattista Donà, appointed *bailo* in 1680, is described by Paolo Preto as belonging to a generation of dynamic and cultivated patricians who revitalized the intellectual life of the Republic.[15] With his knowledge of Turkish, he collected in Istanbul information on flora, fauna, archaeology, and literature. On his return to Venice, he published his *Literature of the Turks*, an original work describing the language, educational system, and cultural and literary production of the Ottoman Empire. Around the same time, his collaborator, dragoman Carli, published the translation of a Turkish history. Donà's circle thus offered new forms of access to Turkish realities and anticipated the attitudes of the eighteenth-century philosophes.

Not all of the ambassadors to Istanbul, however, came through the schools of Padua and the Academy of Venice, and not all of those who did received their entire training in those schools. Two other paths were open to young patricians. They could take up the "practice of merchantry," serving a commercial apprenticeship at one of the Mediterranean ports. That tradition, though on the wane in Venice by the sixteenth century, was carried on by Andrea Gritti—he had studied philosophy at Padua and knew his classics but went to Constantinople to learn the art of commerce—and by Antonio Barbarigo. Or they could enter diplomatic service by joining a relative at one or another of the Venetian embassies. Andrea Gritti had accompanied his grandfather to Spain and to France. Gianfranco Morosini, while still very young, followed Alvise Badoer to Spain. But in either case, the ambassadors continued to be associated with the milieu of high culture and classical education. At least four of them— Marco Minio, Marino Cavalli, and Matteo Zane in the sixteenth century, and Pietro Foscarini in the seventeenth century—were active in the educational reforms at Padua. Antonio Giustiniano,

who between 1502 and 1528 pursued an uninterrupted political
and diplomatic career, had been a lecturer in philosophy and in
theology at Venice. Andrea Gritti, after being elected doge, became one of Venice's greatest patrons of the arts. We know that
Sansovino was his protegé, that he was probably a friend of Titian—who painted a portrait of him—and that he had not only a
taste for music but some musical abilities as well.[16]

The ambassadors to the Porte apparently were familiar with
the books that were being put out by the Venetian presses, and
they read and collected those produced in other Italian cities as
well. One ambassador refers to Machiavelli. Another, without
citing Giovanni Botero, the inventor of the concept of "reasons
of state," uses the categories he introduced into political
thought. The intellectual production of the day is apparent at
every instant in the accounts the ambassadors prepared.

Venice was, however, the site of a paradox. Although knowledge of political philosophy was of great importance to the Venetians, their tradition did not encourage theoretical speculation.
The Venetians were the very first on the Italian peninsula and in
Europe to have shed all doubts as to the autonomy of politics, to
have given God and Caesar their separate due. But having
drawn that line, the Venetians seemed to prefer realism and
pragmatism to abstract creation. As Jakob Burckhardt pointed
out more than century ago, Venice was the silent city. Self-as-
sured, the members of its ruling class did not need to spell
things out among themselves. They shared a political culture
without having to proclaim it, much less question it. Venice was
the city without walls, whose defense lay in the virtue of its
institutions and thus in that of its citizens: steeped in such myths
since as early as the fifteenth century, the Venetians saw their
city as a Platonic republic ruled by sages. In the 1520s, Gasparo
Contarini theorized that outlook in his *De magistratibus et repub-
lica Venetorum*: Venice was the perfect state whose harmony and
civil peace derived from the excellence of its institutions and

laws. It was the perfect society, having avoided both tyranny and rule by the masses by uniting the popular element in the Magior Consiglio, the aristocratic element in the Senate and the Council of Ten, and the monarchical element in the person of the doge.

By reproducing natural hierarchies, the Venetian state was thus in a position to ensure that everyone could "*bene beateque vivere.*" If some were left out, there were many reasons justifying their exclusion, and just as many proving that exclusion did not necessarily mean oppression. Liberty, harmony, and stability were the three pillars on which the city's glory rested. Once this model of the mixed state had been drawn, it was a long time before alterations were required.[17]

In other Italian capitals, political discourse was a distinct genre; not so in Venice. There, it pervaded all aspects of the city's life, was staged in civic rituals, found its way into chronicles and histories, and was expounded publicly before the Senate in the reports the ambassadors brought back from their residence in the great capitals.[18]

These performances were much awaited events, and they became a central ritual of Venetian public life. Ambassadors would return from Rome and from Urbino, from the courts of France and Spain, from the Holy Roman Empire and from the Sublime Porte. Word of a report drew crowds to the Senate. The session demanded long attention: four hours for the report Andrea Gritti presented in 1503; more than four hours of uninterrupted reading for the report Leonardo Donà delivered to the Senate in 1596.

Beginning in 1524, once an ambassador had read his speech, he would turn over the manuscript to the Senate. Although the manuscripts were confidential and were intended to serve the interests of the Serenissima alone, they would circulate: not only in Venice itself—within political circles, among members of the patriciate, who would acquire copies for their libraries—but in the other peninsular capitals as well, and among the courts of

Europe. The number of surviving copies testifies to the success
that some of these reports enjoyed. In 1616 the library at Oxford
owned, among others, those of Marcantonio Barbaro and Giacomo Soranzo from Istanbul and those of Ottavian Valier and
Andrea Zustinian on the Levant. For sale in Rome "at the rate of
fifteen *paoli* per hundred pages" were various reports, including
Marcantonio Barbaro's, Contarini's account of his embassy to
Suleiman in 1535, and reports by Marino Cavalli, Domenico
Trevisan, and Bernardo Navagero.[19]

With its regular rubrics, its almost standardized dimensions,
the ambassador's report became something of a literary genre.
Citizens who did not hold ambassadorial positions and who
therefore were not required to present reports to the Senate
would write them anyway. Three reports from Constantinople
recovered by Albèri—Marcantonio Donini's, Luigi Bonrizzo's,
and Jacopo Ragazzoni's—were the product of what he termed
"the secretarial class." Senator Costantino Garzoni, who had accompanied Ambassador Tiepolo to Spain and later to Constantinople, wrote two for his own pleasure, one from each capital.

In 1589 the ambassadorial reports were given an even wider
circulation with the printing of *Il tesoro politico*. Collected under
that title are "ambassadors' reports, instructions, and assorted
speeches, suitable for gaining knowledge and information about
the states, interests, and dependencies of the world's greatest
princes." The first edition, published in Cologne on behalf of
the Italian Academy, contains seven ambassadorial reports, including, once again, Marcantonio Barbaro's, considered without
a doubt a text of exceptional quality. The report presented by
Maffeo Venier in 1586 would later be added to the collection.
Authors' names were not included in the *Tesoro*, and the texts
themselves underwent some serious alterations, but they formed
nonetheless a sort of manual of political science for the training
and edification of the ruling elite. Italian editions were brought
out one after another, first in Bologna in 1595 and 1598, then in
Milan in 1600. Another edition, presented as the second part to

the *Tesoro*, was published in Bologna in 1603, and a third part appeared in Seravalle in 1605 and was translated into Latin at Frankfurt in 1618. The French translation, *Le trésor politique*, had numerous editions, notably those of 1602 and 1611.[20]

Why did the European elites expend such energy to inform themselves about what was being said in Venice? It was because beyond their masterful displays of oratory, the Venetian ambassadors had perfected an admirable grid through which to observe and read the political realities of their day. Following a codified order, they described and measured the limits of each state, its human, material, and financial resources, its army and its navy; they evaluated the government in power, took inventory of the alliances it maintained, the conflicts in which it was engaged; and they indicated what advantage Venice could gain from the existing situation. The reports offered not daily news, not facts and dates (the dispatches the ambassadors would send in the course of their missions provided these), but careful analysis.

In Venice as elsewhere, there existed on the subject of the Ottoman Empire an entire pamphletary literature devoted to exorcising the fear of a Turkish invasion by prophesying the divine punishment to be visited on the states of the Grand Signor and by announcing his imminent conversion to Christian truth.[21] The ambassadors' reports spoke in a different register. Their goal, pursued with unmistakable rationalist rigor, was more realistic and immediate: to contain the Turkish advance and to defend Venetian positions. Thoughts of conquest may have been entertained, but for the future: the Venetians had no illusions as to the difficulty of embarking on a venture that required concerted action on the part of the Christian princes. In the meantime, one needed to know the enemy, to take stock of the situation, to find the stress points and fault lines where the Ottoman system might weaken of its own account or where Venice— with or without the other Christian powers—might intervene. No theory here, perhaps, but no illusions either: the Venetians knew how to count.

With their wide circulation, the ambassadors' reports helped to shape the European imagination of the day, but the thinking they conveyed was that of the Venetian ruling class. These reports represent the most explicit codification of the Serenissima's political discourse, and it was through their oratory that the Venetian ideal of civic order and the Venetian vision of world order were proclaimed.[22]

The responsibility for upholding the Venetian system belonged to the aristocracy. The young patrician may not have been encouraged to develop a philosophical spirit, but he was certainly expected to serve his homeland. Taking his place in the Great Council at the age of twenty-five, he embarked on a life of political action: in other words, he set out on the *cursus honorum*. Embassies, ordinary and extraordinary, dovetailed with a political career, and no position to which a young patrician might aspire offered more prestige or was more important than that of *bailo* to Istanbul. It was that post, moreover, that produced the greatest number of reports and the most continuous series of them—thirty-nine between 1503 and the end of the sixteenth century, as against twenty-seven describing the situation at the Vatican, twenty-three that of France, and eighteen the affairs of the Holy Roman Empire and Spain.

For a member of the patriciate, the reading of his ambassadorial report was usually one of the critical tests in his career. It was the crowning moment of the mission with which the Senate had charged him. It gave the ambassador the opportunity to show the lucidity of his judgment, to display his culture and eloquence, to prove his knowledge of the world and of men, and to demonstrate that he embodied all the virtues of the political man.[23] Successful completion of a mission to Istanbul paved the way to the highest levels of a political career. Only two exceptions can be found in the long series of ambassadors posted to Istanbul: one of them, Andrea Dandolo, held no further public office after serving as *vice bailo*. The other, Girolamo Lippomano, ended his career ignominiously: to avoid returning to

Venice to face a Senate that had charged him with embezzlement, he threw himself into the sea. But for most of the others, diplomatic careers that took them to Rome, Istanbul, or Spain were followed by government responsibilities in Venice or in its mainland possessions. Andrea Gritti became doge, as did Leonardo Donà. Some not only participated in the day-to-day political life of Venice but played an active role in its revival as well: among the *Giovani* who tried to stop the Republic's decline at the end of the sixteenth century were Leonardo Donà and Ottavio Bon, both of whom had spent time in Istanbul, the former as ambassador extraordinary in 1595, the latter as *bailo* in 1604.[24]

The Venetian patricians thus not only spoke politics, they made it as well. And to make it in ways that might best benefit the Republic, they observed. The senators who assembled to hear a report were not simply providing themselves with a miniaturized spectacle of the world stage, as that ambassador who had returned in 1612 described it; they were lying in wait, as it were, watching the fires flare up in other states, learning at the expense of others what it took to govern well, what weakened empires, how to make peace and wage war.[25] The Serenissima's envoys thus joined in "the effort for knowledge and reason in the interest of self-preservation," in which the Venetian patriciate was tirelessly engaged.[26]

With regard to the Porte, the ambivalence of Venice's policies is well known. By the end of the fifteenth century, Venice had lost its advantage in the Mediterranean and was kept on the defensive by the Turkish navy. But Venice still had essential interests to defend: an important commercial position in the Turkish Empire and in the Levant, possessions in the Mediterranean which were its ports of call along the route to Egypt and Syria. Crete and Corfu, Cyprus—annexed by Venice in 1489—Coron, Modon, and Nauplia in Morea, these formed the maritime frontier that the Turks assailed. They took Coron and Modon in

1503 (while Venice took Zante and Cephalonia), Nauplia in 1540, and Cyprus in 1570. Egypt and Syria fell under Ottoman control in 1516, but Venice wanted to preserve its access to their ports. The Venetians knew that war did not pay. While Europe was entangled in various systems of alliances, Venice did not choose sides. The Venetians were not fanatically obsessed by the idea of a crusade against the infidel. They joined the efforts of other Christian powers only when their own interests were directly threatened. Then, they were the first to seek negotiation, as we see after Lepanto.[27]

The Venetians stood between two seas, two lands, and two blazes. This ambivalence has its most fascinating representative in Andrea Gritti, one of the outstanding figures in Venetian history. We have already seen him, still a young man, discovering the wide world in the company of his grandfather on diplomatic missions in Europe and then in Constantinople, where he learned the merchant's trade. He struck up a friendship with Hersec Ahmet Pasha, who was to become three times grand vizier. Returning to Venice, Gritti married the niece of Doge Vendramin; she died giving birth to Gritti's only legitimate son, Francesco. His four other sons were the children of his Turkish concubine—or concubines. For he had set off again for Istanbul, where he led a life of luxury and knew the principal figures of the Ottoman court. When war broke out between Venice and the Porte in 1499, Gritti was suspected of secret dealings with the leaders of the Venetian army and was put in prison. But thanks to his friends at the court—Sultan Bajazet himself, according to Andrea da Mosto—Gritti was released in 1501 and returned to Venice the following year to participate in the negotiations that Ali Bey had just begun on the sultan's behalf.[28] In 1503 Gritti went back to the Porte, this time as the Republic's orator for the signing of the peace treaty. The report he brought back from this mission is a model of the genre.

In 1523 he was elected doge. His election met with intense resistance. The Venetians, Albèri tells us, had already forgotten his services at the head of the army during the war with the League of Cambrai. Among Venice's lower classes, political opposition found popular expression in verse and song. A poem against Gritti claimed that he "favored the Jews as much as the Christians." It ended with this threat: "If you great ones fail to punish him, the people's hand will slay him." Among the "great ones," it was said that Alvise Priuli, a close relative of Gritti's and one of his great adversaries, had declared that "a man with three bastards in Turkey cannot be doge." Too well disposed toward Jews and too friendly toward Turks. Andrea Gritti and his sons did little to refute this reputation. In 1537 he tried for three entire days to convince the Senate that a diplomatic settlement with the Turks was preferable to war. By a majority vote, the senators opted for war. One of Gritti's two children who were born in Istanbul and whom Gritti brought back with him to Venice, Giorgio, sold all his possessions and returned to Turkey, where he settled permanently.[29] The other, Alvise, who seems to have been dearest to the heart of the old doge, would later attain the highest positions in the Turkish Empire. After pursuing his studies in Venice and Padua like any true member of the Venetian patriciate, Alvise then set off for Istanbul. He made friends with Ibrahim, grand vizier and *beglerbeg* of Rumelia, and Sultan Suleiman's closest companion. Alvise was then made *begoglu*, "godson of the Grand Signor," and keeper of Suleiman's jewels. He amassed a fortune and maintained a court and a seraglio. More than a thousand mouths were fed at his expense. He led the life of a prince—but which kind, Turkish or Venetian? His father spoke Turkish. Certainly Alvise, educated in Italy and versed in the classics, was entirely at ease in Ottoman culture. The sultan had given him the revenues of a Hungarian duchy; he fought alongside the Turks in the Hungarian campaign (1528) and in the siege of Vienna. While his father stood at the helm of the Venetian republic, Alvise was defending the Ottoman cause. In 1530 he commanded the Turkish army that defended Buda against the king of Romania. In 1534 he led an army of three thousand men to Wallachia, Moldavia, and Transylvania. There he was captured by Transylvanian rebels who cut off his head. The doge's biographers write that the death of Alvise affected him more than the untimely death of his only legitimate son in 1506.[30] Perhaps it was Andrea Gritti who earned Venice the reputation of "the Turk's courtesan."[31] Perhaps it was his son. In any case, they were not alone: the ambassadors' reports observe frequently and not without bitterness that Venetian subjects, hoping for rapid promotion in the Turkish army or navy, would convert to Islam and become Turks on their own initiative.

The finest metaphor for Venice's eastern politics, it seems to me, is Antonio Vivaldi's *Juditha triumphans*, composed in 1716. Its message is explicit: it is an *oratorio militare* celebrating the victory of Venice-Judith over the Turk-Holofernes at Corfu in 1716. An oratorio is usually a "sacred drama," a religious work built around a biblical argument and performed in a church to lend force to spiritual exercises. In Venice, if the story was biblical—apocryphal, really—then the allegory was political. Judith, leaving her besieged city to offer herself to Holofernes, sings her first aria about "the sweet hope of freedom." After killing the enemy of her people, she returns to them singing her final aria about the death of the "impious tyrant."[32] Freedom versus tyranny, so much is obvious; but Venice seems to have taken some pleasure in Holofernes' embrace before killing him in his sleep.

Venice knew the enemy. And that knowledge it owed not only to the dispatches its ambassadors sent from Istanbul but also to the observations they brought back with them—precise and rigorous observations, it bears repeating. Had the ambassadors thought it sufficient, however, merely to fill in the standard rubrics of the ambassadorial report with a series of dry entries, the result would have been insufferably monotonous and simply unreadable. But the ambassadors, more politicians than statisticians, were seeking as much to create effects as to produce facts. Consequently, they exploited all resources of rhetoric. One ambassador who had just returned from Istanbul was thanked by the doge for his mission and his report with this comment: "le parole son femine, e li fatti maschi." Let us take this doge at his word and look not only to the hard and virile facts but to the mutable flowers of rhetoric as well. For it is precisely in stylistic devices, lexical departures, metaphors, and various arrangements of motifs that the Venetians best reveal their perceptions of the Ottoman system.

Holofernes

A first series of reports, extending uninterrupted from 1503 to the end of the 1570s, presents a number of significant common features. The period it covers corresponds to the reigns of Bajazet II, Selim I, Suleiman the Magnificent, Selim II, and part of the reign of Murad III. It would be tempting to locate in these reports some of the components of that amalgam from which Montesquieu would later forge the idea of oriental despotism—not only the descriptive traits or "accidental things" that vary from ruler to ruler according to circumstance or personal character, but also what Montesquieu called "distinctive properties," which appeared both constitutive of the system and alien to the values and the principles of a European mind. Yet to locate only those traits would lead to a teleological reading. They do not form a system in themselves, and in the ambassadors' reports they are regularly associated with other structural properties of Ottoman power.

Throughout this first set of reports there runs a persistent ambivalence. The awesome empire of the Grand Signor inspired a fascination that combined admiration and aversion—never sympathy or support, however, for though it was not always said in so many words, the Grand Signor was still the Christians' greatest enemy. There would always be something unacceptable about the power of an infidel ruler who used his colossal force to dominate the Christians; there was no explaining the paradoxical fact that over and over again God should have tolerated and apparently even supported the infidels' victory over his flock. How the Christians could have suffered their reversals at the hands of a militia that had been torn away from the true faith and converted to Islam remained a question without an answer. In 1553, Navagero observed that "this militia considers the Grand Signor's grandeur their own; and though for the most part renegade Christians, they profess greater hatred of the Christians than do the others, and all of them are firmly convinced that if they die in combat against a Christian, they will go straight to Paradise."[33]

Twenty years later, after Lepanto, after that victory that was finally achieved through the unity of the Christians, the paradox of the Turk's usurpation was reformulated once again, by *bailo* Marcantonio Barbaro: "It truly merits serious consideration that the wealth, the power, the government, in short, that the entire state of the Ottoman Empire is founded on and entrusted to people who were all born into the Christian faith and who, by various means, were enslaved and borne off into the Mohammedan sect."[34]

Many of these reports ultimately leave it to the grace of God to lift this punishment from the Christians. In the meantime, the ambassadors track the tensions within the Ottoman system and seek to identify which interventions from without might weaken the infidel.

The fascination was principally a result of the sultan's power. The titles Grand Signor or Grand Turk are used regularly. He is indeed worthy of those titles, and the ambassadors never tire of turning them into superlatives. The very first report in the series declares the Grand Signor to be the world's greatest prince, who presides over the world's most beautiful city and whose fortune surpasses that of all the Christian rulers combined.[35] Marco Minio in 1522 speaks of "la grandissima potenzia di questo Signor," and two years later Pietro Zen speaks of "il grandissimo Signor." Barbarigo, in 1564, concurs: "This Grand Signor is the most powerful."[36] And so do the others. His power derives in the first instance from his territorial resources. Some reports simply list the provinces and kingdoms incorporated into the empire. But the avalanche of names, familiar when they are of places in Europe, more and more exotic toward the east and the south, was enough to create an effect of boundless proportions. Other markers—the superlative to describe the "vastissimo impero dei Turchi,"[37] the emphasis used in designating each part of the whole—signify territorial immensity specifically. The emperor is master of "all" Greece, of "all" Asia Minor, of "all" the confines of the Venetian possessions, of "the whole Mediterranean coast of Asia," of "all the African navies up to the straits of Gibraltar."[38] Some ambassadors stress the number and the diversity of the kingdoms, republics, and provinces the empire had annexed. Others reckon its vast distances, from north to south and east to west. Still others catalogue the borders it shared with such disparate and far-flung kingdoms as Spain, the Holy Roman Empire, Persia, and Abyssinia, the kingdom of Prester John. The empire thus takes on mythic proportions.[39] Sometimes it suffices simply to assert that the empire covers "the three parts of the world"[40] or, more specifically, that "the Grand Signor rules in Asia, in Africa, and in Europe."[41]

A world power, indeed. None of the envoys of the Venetian republic include the Atlantic in their political geographies or take into account the perspectives created by the Great Discoveries. If in assessing the sultan's intentions with respect to the various Christian princes, one or another of the envoys happens to mention Spain or Portugal, it is to compare their forces with those of the Grand Signor in the zones of contact within the old and known world—in the Mediterranean, in the case of Spain; in the Indian Ocean, in the case of Portugal.[42] Even Garzoni, who had traveled widely in the Iberian peninsula a year before his posting to Constantinople, contrasts "the *kingdoms* of the Ponent" with "the very powerful *empire* in the Levant."[43] The center of gravity of the political world, for Venice, still lay within the bounds of the ancient empires.

"E potente di entrata, di gente e di obbedienza," declares Marco Minio in 1522.[44] Revenues, peoples, and obedience: these three foundations of Ottoman power are analyzed relentlessly in subsequent reports. The chapter on the Ottoman state revenues is constantly expanded upon. As with the territories that had come under the Grand Signor's control, the simple enumeration of the various types of taxes, tributes, and ordinary and extraordinary revenues, along with estimates of their return, was sufficient proof of the sultan's wealth. And then there are those heaps of coin-filled leather sacks displayed at the meetings of the council, representing the yield from the land taxes.[45] And which, according to another envoy, did not include the vast quantities of gold hoarded by past emperors[46] or the gifts that pour like rivers into a bottomless chasm.[47] These receipts, writes Garzoni in 1573, "amount to a quasi-infinite sum." The value of the gifts that the sultan receives nearly equals that of the ordinary revenues. He has no less than three "infinitely" filled treasure houses, which Garzoni delights in describing in detail.[48]

The ruler's wealth is augmented further by that of his pashas. The viziers, who receive gifts from all levels of the military and civil hierarchy, amass huge fortunes that revert to the sultan's treasury on their deaths. Under Suleiman, such gifts become so abundant that their display no longer inspires any curiosity. The ambassador, advising his government as to what gifts the Republic might send his majesty, counsels quantity rather than quality, since no one pays attention to them anymore.

All of the reports except one, that of 1562, repeat that revenues exceed expenses: by 30 percent, writes Pietro Zen in 1530; by more than 20 percent, according to Erizzo in 1557; by 47 percent according to Barbarigo's report of the following year; again by 20 percent in the reports from the 1570s. These expenses, too, are described as considerable. The maintenance of the army, however, is financed in part by the country, thanks to the system of the *timar*,[49] again and again held out as a remarkable solution to the problem of supporting troops, a concern of any state. Moreover, the magnitude of court expenditures merely proved how rich the empire really was. In several reports, wondrous descriptions of the seraglio, the fabrics, the jewels, the costumes, the porcelains, the gold and silk carpets, serve to illustrate the abundance that reigned at the Sublime Porte.

Marco Minio's formulation of 1522 evoked the power of human resources, which meant the assurance of revenues from taxation and the regular provision of court, capital, and army both in peacetime and in wartime.[50] In 1573, Garzoni, in discussing Istanbul, explains at length why "this foremost metropolis will never lack what is necessary for the sustenance and comfort of men."[51] On this theme, however, the idea begins to come up during these years that the empire's provinces are emptying of people and that shortages were becoming chronic.[52] We will come back to this decrease in human and material resources later when we consider how the Venetians interpreted it.

To be rich in men, it went without saying, also implied a limitless capacity to raise troops. The chapters on the Turkish army and navy provide detailed descriptions for obvious strategic reasons. The military academies, the assignment of titles and grades, the weaponry employed, the methods of recruitment, training, and advancement, the number of men that could be mobilized—all of the facts and the information needed for the organization of the Venetian defense are brought together. Yet at the same time, the mere mention of such facts was enough to inspire genuine dread in Christian readers. Here and there, of course, the system's imperfections are noted. The arsenal might be found mediocre, or the fleet understaffed. As for the land forces, their weaponry is sometimes deemed inferior to that of the Christians. But all this is presented as though the Ottoman army, by adopting the techniques of its adversaries or by deploying its inexhaustible recuperative powers afforded by an abundance of men and raw materials, could remedy its defects and reestablish its colossal power. For example, even after the destruction of the Turkish navy at Lepanto, Garzoni begins his depiction of the Ottoman military in these terms: "This most powerful emperor's forces are of two kinds, those of the sea and those of the land, and both are terrifying."[53] After describing the army and the fleet at considerable length, he concludes that the latter is still able to "travagliare la cristianità tutta," to torment all of Christendom.[54]

"All the best conditions that one might wish in a great and invincible army, all, I believe, can be found in the soldiers of this signor," writes Dandolo in 1562. The number of soldiers, superior to that of all the Christian princes, their virtue, their experience, the knowledge of warfare displayed by officers and the rank and file alike, their courage, their unity, such are the qualities that this ambassador brings out. The men act "of a single will for the public good": coming from a Venetian, this assessment cannot be taken lightly. *Unanimitas* was one of the central values of the Venetian political ideal. Other ambassadors attest to the thrift and the perseverance of the Turkish fighters, still others to the discipline and impeccable order of the army on campaign. For all of them the key word is "obedience." It conjured up all at once images of the army's organization, the troops' discipline, the men's absolute devotion to the emperor.[55] We will come back to this in a moment.

As a result of the enormous power of the empire and its army, the Grand Turk "holds in his hands the keys to all Christendom, such that he could easily penetrate the Christians' entrails," states Marco Minio in 1522. "Henceforth," he writes, "all Christendom should fear incurring a great extermination."[56] Menacing, fearsome, invincible power: it is a leitmotif of the ambassadorial reports. "They are the greatest fighters in the world," writes Cavalli in 1560; they are to be feared, not fought. The Grand Signor has so much territory, land, and obedient men at his disposal, says Barbarigo in 1564, that "these three elements alone make him invincible."[57] In 1573, two years after Lepanto, Barbaro wonders again whether the Ottoman Empire might not become the universal monarchy. He is not indulging in some facile turn of oratory, intended to lend a note of stridency and resonance to the opening lines of his report. Rather, he is demonstrating why Venice was henceforth the primary target of Turkish expansion, the next victim of its imminent advance.[58] A few years later, Tiepolo reiterates: there is good reason to believe that Murad III can threaten the entire world and, at the first attack, the empire and Venice. It would be vain, he writes, absolutely vain, to think that such an empire could be brought down by human hands alone.[59]

In the Heart of
the Seraglio

This empire, which gave "all the world's princes, especially the Christian ones on its borders, understandable cause for terror," was based not on mere strength of numbers nor on sheer force.[60] It relied on a political order as well. This was the principal object of the Venetian observers' fascination: a system in which every part was subordinate to the center in a relation of mutual tension, a structure that united all the levels of the hierarchy while making each of them dependent on the top. The Ottoman Empire formed an imposing construction whose architecture seemed to conform to the canons of beauty set down by Palladio. It obeyed a single logic, which accounted for both its material power and its relentless territorial expansion. In whatever they describe, the sessions of the Divan, the regular ceremonies of court, the special ceremonies for the reception of an ambassador, or the institution of the seraglio, the Venetian ambassadors see the same logic at work, achieving a perfect orchestration and a complete mobilization of energies in the service of the sultan's grandeur.

Let us follow Bernardo Navagero into the four seraglios of the Grand Signor Suleiman the Magnificent.[61] The year is 1533. The seraglios are those of Andrianople, Constantinople, and Pera, and the sultan's own. Whenever a war occurs on land or at sea, Navagero tell us, the seraglios fill up with Christian children. Fourteen nations, he says, from the Russians to the Spaniards, have provided children for the Grand Turk. Without pressing the matter—no lamentations here for the fate of the little ones or for their families, a cherished theme with Christian writers—Navagero manages to explain that one of the empire's motives for maintaining a permanent state of war is to furnish the seraglio with young recruits. Navagero does not say that the children are immediately made slaves; rather, he indicates their fate elliptically, for soon he begins referring to them as such. They are divided among the first three seraglios, he writes, are dressed from head to toe in new clothes, and are entrusted to the care of Turkish masters who every day until evening teach them language, writing, and reading, and "give them to understand their law"—a novel understatement meant to convey that they are converted to Islam. At nightfall, when the masters leave the seraglio, the little ones are placed under a guard of white eunuchs and "Saracens" (read "blacks"). Navagero carefully specifies the echelons of the hierarchy through which the masters can rise to attain the honored rank of *mufti*, or leader of Turkish Islam, and he indicates the cost of each rank. He gives a similar account for the hierarchy of seraglio eunuchs.

As for the young charges, whom Navagero now refers to as pages, they are given one *aspre* a day. And after two years of training, the *capi-agà*, who supervises all the seraglios, comes and inspects the boys one by one and picks out those whose beards have begun to grow. They are now *spahis*, and with their new title, their pay increases to between ten and twelve *aspres* a day. From the products of this first selection, those who are most beautiful in body and manners, those who have distinguished themselves in their studies or whom luck has favored are set apart and sent to the seraglio of his majesty. There they are placed under the guard of twenty white eunuchs, four of whom are the highest-ranking members of their corps and enjoy the title, the pay, and the regular gifts their position entails. The other eunuchs receive ten to fifteen *aspres* per day, "in addition to their clothing, all of which is of silk and gold."

Then comes the description of the seraglio of the Grand Signor with its five houses. In the first, or "small," house live the youngest pages, who are between six and fourteen years old; they learn to write Arabic, Turkish, and Persian and train at archery. The second, or "great," house is home to pages from the age of fifteen to the "age of virility," who practice the same arts. Younger and older pages are all paid eight *aspres* per day—like the religion instructors assigned to the first three seraglios—and though their garments are of a cloth "that is not of the first quality," their caps are made of golden cloth from Bursa. The third house, where the great chamberlain lives, houses three to four hundred pages who learn archery, combat, jumping, and running. The fourth house is called the *caznà*, and this is where the great treasurer lives, along with sixty pages. When an employee from the treasury has to make a withdrawal, he is accompanied by several of these pages, "who stand in a line, holding each other's hands, neither gesturing nor speaking to each other," until the employee has formulated his demand, and then they instantly comply. These pages receive the same salary as others, eight *aspres* a day, but they wear satin, damask, and gold cloth from Bursa, and their caps are worth one hundred to one hundred fifty *sequins*.

The fifth house, whose Turkish name means "the most perfect chamber," is the sultan's own. Twenty-five or thirty pages live there with him, five or six of whom stand perfectly still day and night, without lifting their heads or uttering a word. While his majesty sleeps, four of them keep watch, two by two, sitting beneath a torch of white wax which burns throughout the night, and, wrapped in a sable pelisse if the night is cold, they keep a book beside them to stay awake. The guard maintains its vigil, says Navagero, not to protect the sultan from some enemy, but to assist him should he want to say his prayers or attend to some other need. The pay of these pages goes up to thirty *aspres* a day. They wear very fine damask, satin, and gold cloth, and their embroidered belts are worth one hundred fifty to two hundred *sequins* each. Three of them are singled out as favorites: one bears the Grand Signor's bow and arrow and his sword, the second his change of clothes, the third his eating utensils. These three pages can advance through the ranks and, through actions or simply good fortune, can become *sanjakbeg, aga* of the janissaries, *beglerbeg* of the land or of the sea, and even grand vizier.

Finally, every two years the pages are replaced by another group. The four great eunuchs described earlier come to select those pages who are showing the first growth of beard. From these, they choose the most beautiful, the most literate, the most "costumati"—those who have acquired the best manners—for the fourth house and for the perfect chamber. The *capi-agà* then announces to the sultan that the time for the relief has arrived. "The sultan says *nolà*, which means 'so be it,'" and at once all "the bearded ones" line up to kiss the hand of the sultan, who is at the doorway of the house, on a small square that has been covered in the richest carpeting of silk and gold, seated *alla turchesca*, cross-legged, with great majesty, one hand on his hip, the other on the piles of carpet. And he beckons to the bearded ones, who come before him silently, one by one, and, full of cheer and with great respect, they kiss his hand or his foot. After thanking God and his majesty for being able to leave the seraglio in good health, they are divided up among various captains and begin to learn to live life on the outside. Their pay varies between fifteen and one hundred and fifty or two hundred *aspres*, depending on the house from which they have just come.

The four seraglios are thus a school, a formidable machine for the selection of talent and the training of bodies and minds. The institution raises its youth in unanimous and exclusive devotion to the emperor. They learn not to submit to order but rather to be its artisans. Education becomes a perpetual celebration of imperial grandeur; gestures, sounds, and costumes are predetermined as meticulously as in a ballet. Order, silence, chastity, education in religious law; to which we might add that the janissaries call one another "brother" and that their rallying cry is

"Padiscià," "Emperor our father." Navagero's description obviously seeks to evoke a monastic discipline. After him others abbreviate: the seraglios, they write, are the Turks' monasteries.[62]

In the recruitment and the promotion of janissaries the same impeccable order is observed, which, for Navagero and several others who follow him, consists of discipline, unity, and virtue. Navagero also describes the perfect organization of the four weekly sessions of the Porte. He offers the sight of an assembled army about to set off for new conquest. At the court as well as in the country, the deployment of men, always in impressive numbers, takes place seamlessly amid the rustle of uniforms and feathered caps, the splendor of steeds and weaponry, the absolute silence of the troops.[63]

Navagero's presentation is not confined to a purely empirical register. Beyond his careful depiction of the parts that constitute the system in its entirety, the idea he seeks to convey is that of a perfect machine in which every part has its place. Each element is measured, ordered, named, and precisely situated in a strict configuration. Everyone works together to serve the grandeur of the Signor, and all benefit from it, his material and symbolic gratification sanctioning the role each actor is called on to play.

The result of this majestic force is that all men, civilian and soldier alike, share in the imperial splendor, to which there are two sides.[64] One is the absolute submission of the subjects at all levels of the social pyramid. The other is the sovereign's authority, which, for its part, is no less absolute.

The people are directly subject to the sultan's authority because there are no other lords besides the sultan himself. This theme of the absence of an aristocracy and other intervening bodies first appears in 1534 in De Ludovisi's report.[65] Montesquieu, in the eighteenth century, will put it this way: "Without a nobility and without a monarchy, one has a despot." The sixteenth century, however, had not yet begun to speak of despotism. What is stressed instead is that the absence of aristocratic families eliminates the risk of political subversion and that "there

is no small advantage, and no less security, in letting distinguished families succeed one another in government."[66] Consequently, "all of these peoples are so many slaves at his mercy, so
forsaken and so ruined that there remains no one with any
strength or vigor."[67] That to deprive men of their freedom is to
deprive them of their energy is a motif taken up in many reports, for it pointed to a site of possible intervention against the
Ottoman Empire: the subject Christian populations should greet
as liberators the first armies to come free them from its yoke.[68]
That, at least, was the hope. For it was impossible to overlook
the fact that Greeks and even some Venetian subjects had abandoned their homes or their ships to enter the sultan's service of
their own volition. One ambassador even advises that boys under sixteen years old not be allowed aboard ship, because they
would not know how to withstand the temptation to become
Turks.[69]

But at all events, whether or not they willingly accept their
servitude, the sultan's subjects obey. "Obedience, considered by
all to be the most solid foundation for any empire, maintains
this one without a doubt."[70] Several explanations are offered for
this obedience. It may be that the subjects—slaves in fact if not
by law—have become servile, the abject nature of the slave being such that it is his inclination to obey. Or it may be that the
fear inspired in them by the exercise of power has made them
docile. As for the slaves who have grown up in the palace, they
become the children of the Grand Signor, his *figlioli*, and thus
owe him the obedience that is a father's due. And finally, the
absolute submission to the Grand Signor derives from the hopes
for promotion which the system permits. In the absence of a
hereditary aristocracy, lightning ascents are possible, either
through the selection and training of talent, as described above,
or by the sultan's will alone. Slavery is not without its advantages.[71] In the eyes of the Venetians, the submission of those
who are in the emperor's service is "incredible" and "unaccountable," in that it is voluntary and not imposed.[72] And this is as

true for the simplest foot soldier as it is for the grand vizier. The ambassadors take some pleasure in recounting the unaccountable—for example, how the pashas, on learning of their disgrace, docilely come before the executioner and offer him their heads rather than disobey their master by fleeing for their lives. The ambassadors vie with one another in repeating that for the Turks there is no greater glory than that of calling themselves the slaves of the Grand Signor.[73]

From the ruler's standpoint, this relation signified his absolute authority, his power of life and death over each of his subjects regardless of the position to which they had climbed. But was it arbitrary authority? Not necessarily. Several sultans display the justice and the wisdom befitting a prince. Their wisdom is a consequence of their education and the practice of letters. In 1503 Gritti sketches the first portrait of an Ottoman sultan: Bajazet was once thought humane, he writes, but now that opinion has changed, for he took the life of an altogether excellent man to whom he had been very close and who deserved the best that the Ottoman house could offer, for the simple reason that this particular pasha had become too powerful, and that offended him. Yet Gritti, apparently conceding that supreme authority is not something to be shared, speaks of the prince's cruelty as though it were a matter of opinion rather than a matter of fact. Twice he stresses the "very great humaneness" Bajazet brings to negotiations.[74] With his grasp of philosophy and his great knowledge of cosmography, Bajazet comes across as a man in whom the Venetian is pleased to recognize a humanistic wisdom. Selim, described in his turn by Ambassador Mocenigo, is a "just" man, an assiduous reader of *The Life of Alexander*, whose exploits he seeks to imitate so as to become master of the world. This signor "is just," says Marco Minio in 1527; he is reputed to be a philosopher and spends many hours in study. Minio is speaking about Suleiman—whom posterity will remember as the Magnificent and the Ottomans as the Legislator. Subsequent portraits of him that the ambassadors offer over the course of his long reign, which lasted from 1520 to 1566, return constantly to the theme of his wisdom: he is a man of his word who commits no wrong, providing he is well informed; he is a very religious man who observes the laws of his faith; he reads the exploits of Alexander and Persian history and is nourished by the glorious examples of the past. One can see the wisdom on his face, which has a "marvelous grandeur and a sweetness that makes him pleasing to the eyes of all who behold him."[75]

After the reign of Selim II (1566–1574), generally painted in darker tones, Murad III appears to have reestablished princely justice. Devoting himself "to the study of law and history, he is much inclined to govern with justice."[76]

Now Selim, the first prince to be described as just, was in fact suspected of having come to power by poisoning his father. Not so, writes Mocenigo—there is no basis to the rumor.[77] And if Selim did have Janus Pasha and his own brother-in-law killed, Mocenigo provides three reasons to explain those measures. The prince's severity is thereby justified. Similarly, the ambassadors continue to find Suleiman "very just and very wise" even after he ordered the assassination of Ibrahim Pasha, his childhood friend, confidant, and grand vizier, in 1536, and later that of his eldest son and heir apparent, Prince Mustafa, who was loved by the entire army. Only Donini, in 1562, observes that Suleiman, with his reputation as a just prince, also deserves after 1553 "to be called the cruelest and most irreverent father, who has stained his hands with his own blood by having had put to death his first-born son Mustafa," then Mehemet, and finally Bajazet and four of Bajazet's sons who had fled to Persia, his fifth son having been murdered in the empire itself.[78] Later ambassadors, unmoved by Donini's report, continue to speak of the great sultan's vast wisdom. If he ordered all those people put to death, it was because they challenged his authority. A fitting retribution.

More than natural inclinations and literary pursuits, what made for a just prince, in the eyes of the ambassadors, was his intimate knowledge and strict application of the law. The Venetian ambassadors stress that in the Ottoman Empire there was indeed a law, the law of Islam. *Legge* and *fede* were interchangeable. In a nonsecularized system of thought, religion remained the only foundation for the law. And if the Moslem religion was repugnant to Christians, it nonetheless provided an order, an ethos, for ruler and subjects alike. This "law" is what mobilized the subjects, gave them the courage and the desire to die in battle against the Christians. It promoted devotion to the public good, and so the Venetians found observed at the Porte one of the central values of their own culture.[79] As for the ruler, if he was a man of his faith, he was a man of honor. Suleiman is thus a just and clement prince because he is "a perfect Turk"—read, "a good Moslem"—"religiosissimo nella sua legge [deeply religious in his law]," or, again, "grandissimo riguardatore della sua legge [a great observer of his law]."[80]

Certain reports speak of his predecessor, Selim I, as "having a very cruel face, and cruel he is indeed."[81] The reason is that in governing, Selim disregards the law. Descriptions of Suleiman's successor, Selim II, tend toward the horrific. "He dyes the edges of his eyelids black. Some would have it that he does it for hygienic reasons, while others say that it is to inspire dread in whoever looks at him, which I would dispute were it not for the rest of his actions which also show him thus inclined."[82] Selim may well be a poet, a man who addresses his grand vizier in verse.[83] But by transgressing his religion's prohibitions and giving himself over to drink, he ceases to be a man of faith, literally and figuratively.

The Venetians thus acknowledge an order visible in each of the practices of the court and the army; a law shared by ruler and subject alike; a wisdom on which the prince's authority was founded. They note the contradictory play of forces in the various wheels of the imperial machinery, the opposing sides to each piece in that machinery, but in the end they find rationality in it. That subjects can be slaves is inconceivable for the Venetians—they themselves may accommodate domestic servitude

on their own soil and are still active in the slave trade, but they
see no contradiction, because the law grants citizenship to men
of Venetian birth—but the servitude of the Turks they understand as the condition on which their devotion to the state de-
pended. The sultan's cruelty is horrendous, but because it guar-
antees the obedience of the subjects, the lowly along with the
mighty, it ensures political stability. Authority can be led astray
when the ruler turns his power over to his grand vizier, but no
matter how powerful the latter might become, he is shadowed
by the possibility of disgrace. Between the mortal menace that
the sultan holds over his head and the rivalry of the other
pashas, the vizier is held in check and thus is bound to respect
the law and to serve the Grand Signor's interests with unfailing
rigor. Civic harmony and peace and devotion to the state, values
central to the Venetian ethos, are thus found among the Turks as
well, though they attain these values by methods different from
those of the Republic.

The Venetian observers are put off, however, by some of the
practices they encounter. To them, these practices seem marked
by insoluble contradiction. Sooner or later, they are bound to
undermine the empire. First, there is the uncertainty of the
transfer of power. There is indeed a "house" of Osman, a dynasty of undivided authority, but one never knows with cer-
tainty which son of the reigning sultan will succeed him. Parri-
cides and fratricides attend every ascension to the throne, giving
rival factions in the army and the seraglio the occasion to display
their violence.[84]

A second custom that makes the empire the anti-Venice: the
regulation of the entire system derives less from respect for law
than from personal attachments to the sultan's glory and fears of
his retribution. Hence that paradox of the sultan's officers whose
fate it is to serve him unquestioningly as long as he uses his
power justly. But what happens when his authority is perverted?
When religious law is disregarded, the sultan is debased. When
he neglects his faith, he ceases to be a man of honor and is sub-

ject only to his own caprices. The system recognizes no natural aristocracy—whether based on noble lineage or on nobility of character—and therefore it lacks such social constraints as could temper a prince's degeneracy. That lack is especially felt when the sultan withdraws from his own dignitaries to keep company with the most abject of men. It is staggering, writes Erizzo in 1557, to see what type of men he communes with in his apartments, "where no one is permitted but eunuchs, mutes, and other men of the most abject varieties, who are his slaves. For men of his own stature never enter there, they speak to the Signor only during his ceremonies and in very public places."[85] In 1573, Garzoni writes derisively of Selim's predilection for dwarfs and jesters and of his affection for one of his mutes, while Marcantonio Barbaro criticizes those Ottoman emperors in the habit of withdrawing from the commerce of men, speaking only to eunuchs, pages, and women, all of whom are ignorant in worldly matters, having been raised in the seraglios isolated from the outside.[86]

Here we can grasp the reservations of the members of the Venetian patriciate: their sense of pride in belonging to a legitimate elite made them balk at the absence of an Ottoman nobility and at the way base plebeians could rise to power. If the inversion of social roles was not based on merit and devotion, how could it be justified? Yet, in Europe, the royal courts had never lost their fondness for jesters, dwarfs, and fools, who continued to be regarded as purveyors of truth and wisdom. The European aristocracy still took great delight in listening to the singing of *castrati*, who by the second half of the seventeenth century had become a regular feature in the churches of Italy. Yet all this was unacceptable at the Sublime Porte. Why? Beings such as these had a place, and that place was not in the seat of power and political action. A painting from the end of the sixteenth century by Agostino Carracci portrays "Arrigo the hairy, Pietro the fool, Amon the dwarf and other beasts": they were, as a matter of fact, at the court of Cardinal Farnese, but as curiosities of nature, a collection of specimens in a zoo.[87] In Venice, Veronese was brought before the Inquisition in 1573. He had just completed a *Last Supper* for the refectory at the SS. Giovanni e Paolo monastery. A jester and his parrot, a dwarf, and a dog appear in the painting. Why these characters? asked the inquisitor. "For decoration," the painter replied. Did it seem fitting to him to associate the Last Supper of our Lord with jesters, dwarfs, and other ridiculous subjects? "My lord, no." Veronese admitted his error but defended his work by pointing out that the characters were on the margins of the painting, "outside the space where the Supper took place," and that he had respected the rules that the most prestigious painters followed. The painting was ultimately unchristened and would be called simply *Feast in the House of the Levi*.[88]

The story is exemplary, an indication of a certain distance that had to be maintained. It was one thing for the sultan to amuse himself with subhuman creatures, but for him to neglect the conduct of his affairs and isolate himself in such company was to turn the normal order of things upside down.

Finally, a third disorder prompting the ambassadors' aversion: everything—decisions, ranks, politics itself—had a price. The Venetians, of course, were masters in the arts of commerce. Buying and selling, counting and paying—these things they did. But within the confines of the marketplace. Did money enter into political affairs? Yes, but according to a logic that to the Venetians appeared quite different from that of the Turks. In Venice, decisions were governed by principles. Election and advancement followed an independent political logic: whoever proved his civic worth received recognition and reward in the political domain. Within the civic space, a dignitary, a citizen in his country's service, gave not only of himself but of his fortune as well. He spent in order to maintain his standing, to give manifest signs of his dignity: the presents he took with him when he set out on a mission, the suit of clothing he wore, the handouts he distributed upon his election, the patronage he offered—all this liberality was the measure of his power. Such ostentation did not expect repayment. Handouts were a kind of potlatch: one gave to the people without keeping count, without knowing the beneficiaries' names; one gave with a blind generosity, without regard for cost. One gave to those less important than oneself, for the greater glory of the Republic. To represent Venice with anything less than splendor would be to demean her. If there were rewards in such largesse, they were symbolic and benefited the Republic itself. This is what is called magnificence.

At the Sublime Porte, everything happened the other way around. Ministers, governors, judges, lower-grade officers, everyone got presents and money; services rendered or merely promised had to be paid for. One received from those below and gave to those above, and thus the top of the social pyramid was choked with gifts. In contrast again to Venice, a man's power was measured by the volume of gifts he received.[89] Sultans and viziers, it is true, were capable of great largesse. They lived handsomely, built mosques, and endowed public institutions. But they also expected abundant gifts. As the rules governing promotions and compensation for services were such that one could never be certain who would hold the highest offices, the Serenissima's representatives had to garner favors from individuals of all sorts. And in the absence of both a hereditary social hierarchy and a rigid institutional hierarchy, "the wheel of fortune" could at any moment raise a subject up from obscurity. Which meant that the Venetians had to face what was for them the intolerable constraint of having to bestow gifts on those less important than they in order to obtain some advantage—immediate or deferred—from the highest echelons. When one had to stoop to give, it was called corruption. "In Constantinople," writes Erizzo in 1557, "one has to lavish respect and favors on everyone, even on the *marioli* [those adventurers originally from Candia and other islands who were rounded up in the taverns and enlisted into the Ottoman navy] because there is a perpetual wheel of fortune that the Signor causes to rise and fall according to the spins of his caprice."[90]

It should be noted that in both Venice and Turkey "it is by bankrupting oneself"—or at least by going to great expense—"that one accedes to power."[91] In both places, expenditure had political results as its aim (something no longer considered acceptable). There were rumblings in Venice when Doge Andrea Gritti was slow to make the customary handouts after his election. But in Istanbul and Venice, the beneficiaries of the largesse occupy opposite positions. And so in this respect, too, for the Serenissima's ambassadors, the Porte is the anti-Venice.

The Prophecy of Daniel

The Venetians generally called a spade a spade, especially when
it could be called a European kind of spade. They named and
spelled people and things in keeping with the codes of their day.
Ambassadors, in particular, knew their political geography like
the backs of their hands, and none of the nuances of the various
princely honorifics escaped them. In Poland the monarch was a
king, in Muscovy a duke, in Persia a *sofi*; "Caesar" meant the
emperor, and the "most Christian king" was obviously the king
of France. Foreign institutions they presented using a system of
equivalences understood by their contemporaries, and when the
need arose they translated exotic facts into Italian. The Grand
Turk, Erizzo tells us in 1557, was commonly called "Cunchiar"
in Turkish, "Sultan" in Arabic, "Hem" in Tartar, "Sciach" in Persian, "all of which words in our language mean 'emperor'; but
those who wish to call him by his true name call him 'Patisci-
ach,' which, in our language, sounds greater than 'Emperor.'
And they call the emperor 'Spain,' or, simply, 'Charles.'"[92]
Although sensitive to the weight of words, the ambassadors de-
parted from the practice of strict translation and felt free to use
anachronisms when speaking of the Turkish Empire. To designate its eastern regions, they often turned to an archaic to-
ponymy or made it a point to recall the ancient kingdoms behind the new names. Navagero, in 1553, calls the Iraqi provinces
"Mesopotamia," includes among the Grand Signor's possessions
the "kingdoms of the Assyrians and the Medes," and speaks of

"Babylon, which they call Baghdad."[93] Similarly, Morosini, in 1585, counts not Baghdad but Babylon among the eastern provinces.[94] Yet the site of Babylon is some eighty kilometers from Baghdad.

Reminders of Alexander crop up as well. In 1583, Paolo Contarini found telltale signs of the decline of the empire. Yet he emphasizes its territorial immensity and its recent expansion at the expense of Persia, explaining that the Turks had just taken the Iron Gate built by Alexander.[95] In particular, the sultan seemed to reincarnate the great general. Early sixteenth-century descriptions give us a Selim steeped in *The Life of Alexander*—a chivalric romance in Persian and in Turkish which was much the vogue throughout the East and among European readers, too, in translation. Selim, writes one ambassador, sought to imitate Alexander and conquer Asia, Africa, and Europe, thus making himself master of the world.[96] Suleiman, his successor, is said to have found his models in both Alexander and the Persians, and to the same effect.[97]

The Turks, it was repeatedly suggested, were heirs to the great empires of the past. Not only had they absorbed most of the known kingdoms of antiquity, but the virtues of the Roman legions were now theirs. The order, the discipline, the abhorrence of blasphemy and games of chance in the Ottoman army, the religious respect for the emperor, were always spoken of with favorable reference to the Roman model, whereas the insubordination rampant in the armies of Christendom was denounced.[98] Having retaken one by one the countries that had once been within the Roman orbit, the Ottoman army seemed to resurrect the imperial project; better, it seemed capable of extending its borders even farther.[99]

And finally, Istanbul was always called Constantinople, was compared over and over again to Rome, and continued to be looked upon as the sometime capital of the Roman Empire.[100]

Why this archaeological vision of the Ottoman Empire, as though it were merely the uppermost layer in a thick stratigraphy? Why, Byzantine heritage and Asiatic genealogy aside, establish a filiation between the Ottomans and certain moments from the past—and only those? The Medes, the Assyrians, the Persians, Alexander, and Rome were signals read by the Venetian ambassadors on the map of the world, signals that in their turn they sent on to their contemporaries.

For there was meaning in history; it had a direction, a design, a destination. The sixteenth century had not yet abandoned imperial expectations. An emperor would appear and usher in the second coming of Christ. As the Middle Ages came to an end, various prophecies had expressed this hope, each proposing its own candidate: now a French ruler, now a German one, was called upon to establish this empire. And in every case, it was to be a universal empire. It was characteristic, for example, for Charles VIII, entering Naples in 1495, to have himself acclaimed king of France, emperor of Constantinople, and king of Jerusalem.[101]

Indeed, Orient and Occident had to be reunited. Who among the Christians—Rome, the emperor, or France—would accomplish the undertaking? And what if it were Venice? The fourteenth century had had its Andrea Dandolo to champion the idea of a government concentrated in the hands of a prince—contrary to the Venetian tradition that, as doge, Dandolo had embodied. The peoples' fortunes, whether good or ill, would depend on the prince alone, who would enjoy absolute power, even over the church. This ideal, once realized by Constantine, had not outlived the emperor. To the Venetian prince it fell to profit from the *translatio imperii*, because nowhere on the horizon, neither in the east nor in the west, was there a new Constantine in sight.[102]

And what if it were the emperor of the infidels, as it seemed God might allow? What the Venetian ambassadors read, not only in the power and expansion of the Ottomans but also in their resurrection of the great empires of the past, was a vocation for world domination, which the Venetians saw not merely as a military and political accomplishment but as the fulfillment of an eschatological project.

Another medieval tradition saw the Moslems as the antithesis of Christianity and associated them with the Antichrist. An apocalyptic image of Islam fueled the fear of a Christendom encircled, though Christianity's besiegement was thought perhaps to be the harbinger of the new Kingdom of God.[103] In the sixteenth century one biblical text enjoyed great popularity and was subjected to various interpretations. That text was the Prophecy of Daniel. The Venetians knew the story: Nebuchadnezzar, king of Babylon, has a dream that no one on earth seems able to understand. Young Daniel is brought in before the king and solves the riddle. This is what he says:

> *To you, O king, as you lay in bed came thoughts of what would be hereafter, and he who reveals mysteries made known to you what is to be. But as for me, not because of any wisdom that I have more than all the living has this mystery been revealed to me, but in order that the interpretation may be made known to the king, and that you may know the thoughts of your mind.*
>
> *You saw, O king, and behold, a great image. This image, mighty and of exceeding brightness, stood before you, and its appearance was frightening. The head of this image was of fine gold, its breast and arms of silver, its belly and thighs of bronze, its legs of iron, its feet partly of iron and partly of clay. As you looked, a stone was cut out by no human hand, and it smote the image on its feet of iron and clay, and broke them in pieces; then the iron, the clay, the bronze, the silver, and the gold, all together were broken in pieces, and became like the chaff of the summer threshing floors; and the wind carried them away, so that not a trace of them could be found. But the stone that struck the image became a great mountain and filled the whole earth. This was the dream; now we will tell the king its interpretation.*
>
> *You, O king, the king of kings, to whom the God of heaven has*

given the kingdom, the power, and the might, and the glory, and into whose hand he has given, wherever they dwell, the sons of men, the beasts of the field, and the birds of the air, making you rule over them all—you are the head of gold. After you shall arise another kingdom inferior to you, and yet a third kingdom of bronze, which shall rule over all the earth. And there shall be a fourth kingdom, strong as iron, because iron breaks to pieces and shatters all things; and like iron which crushes, it shall break and crush all these. And as you saw the feet and toes partly of potter's clay and partly of iron, it shall be a divided kingdom; but some of the firmness of iron shall be in it, just as you saw iron mixed with the miry clay. And as the toes of the feet were partly iron and partly clay, so the kingdom shall be partly strong and partly brittle. As you saw the iron mixed with miry clay, so they will mix with one another in marriage, but they will not hold together, just as iron does not mix with clay. And in the days of those kings the God of heaven will set up a kingdom which shall never be destroyed, nor shall its sovereignty be left to another people. It shall break in pieces all these kingdoms and bring them to an end, and it shall stand for ever; just as you saw that a stone was cut from a mountain by no human hand, and that it broke in pieces the iron, the bronze, the clay, the silver, and the gold. A great God has made known to the king what shall be hereafter. The dream is certain, and its interpretation sure. (Daniel 2:29–45; RSV 2d ed.)

"This was the dream." The text became the basis for the theory of four monarchies as phases of world history, which held that the pagan kingdoms—Babylonian-Assyrian, Persian, Greek, and Roman—were to be succeeded by the ultimate establishment of the Kingdom of God on earth. Taken up again by Carion and Melanchthon, this notion had considerable importance among the German Protestant humanists.[104] According to historian F. E. Manuel, prior to Hegel and Marx it was the prophecy of the four kingdoms that "had seen the most books produced within the confines of its grand design."[105]
Did this prophecy have currency in Venice? Did the fantasy

find an echo among the Venetian ambassadors, their rationalist rigor notwithstanding? It is more than plausible that it did. Rabbi Isaac Abravanel, around the end of the fifteenth century, identified the Turkish Empire as the last monarchy. His work, first published in 1551, was translated into Latin and thereupon became, Manuel points out, "a focus of learned controversy" among Christians.[106] Around 1517 the prophecy of Francesco Meleto spread through Florence, was published, and found an audience on the peninsula. Basing his prophecy on the Book of Daniel, this son of a Florentine-Bolognese merchant and a Russian serf was inspired by conversations he had had in the course of business travels to Constantinople with Jews and Moslems. He announced the imminent conversion of the Jews and the Moslems alike and the renewal of the church. All of this was to be followed by universal salvation and an era of peace and happiness.[107] In 1570, in Venice itself, Agostino Ferentilli published his *Discorso universale*, being, as its subtitle goes on to say, a discussion of the six ages and the four monarchies, and at the conclusion of which "it is shown by means of a diligent temporal calculation how long the present century will last, following the opinion of Elia, rabbi, and that of Latantio Firmiano." Conversations with Jews and Moslems in the one instance, the reckonings of a cabalist rabbi in the other: these are vivid indications of an effervescence that reached beyond the Catholic or Protestant worlds.

It was also in Venice that another book was printed, Giovanni Tarcagnota's *Delle istorie del mondo*, in which the author, writing what was obviously intended as a universal history, relates Nebuchadnezzar's dream and Daniel's interpretation, structuring his historical material around this myth.[108] Other authors, whose traces we will not take up here, do likewise. To be sure, these chronologists did not situate the Ottoman Empire at the end of time. But they did help to establish the model of a finite history, with its successive phases marked by the four empires.

Finally, there was the very famous book by Guillaume Postel,

De la république des Turcs. After a long sojourn in Constantinople in the 1530s, and two stays in Venice between 1547 and 1549 and then in 1555, Postel published a remarkably rich description of the Turkish Empire which met with great success. In Turkey he found a model for universal monarchy and sought the reasons for its exceptional success. The Turks, he says, "conquested" the lands they held with "sobriety, patience, and obedience, or, in a word, military discipline." The Turks applied themselves "to their conquests with a more-than-Hannibalesque skill, surpassing all others in holding on to what they had won." One had to know them, he wrote, if one was to emulate them. Postel, who first proposed the universal monarchy to the emperor, dedicates this work to the dauphin, for he has now concluded that it has fallen to France to use the Turk's own weapons against him and establish a universal monarchy on behalf of Christianity, the world's only rightful sovereign.[109]

It is within this debate of eschatological proportions that everything the ambassadors said about the perfect political structure of the great seraglio, the organization of the army, and the vastness of the empire must be understood. Marcantonio Barbaro formulated the threat most explicitly, but it is an underlying theme in other accounts contemporary and subsequent to his. Although writing in 1573, two years after Lepanto, he nonetheless begins his account with these words: "Most serene prince and excellent lords, since, by the will of God, the Ottoman emperor has in the course of continuing victories seized so many provinces and brought so many kingdoms under his yoke and, in so doing, has made the whole world fear him, it is not beyond reason to wonder if he might not finally go so far as to establish a universal monarchy."[110]

The dazzled descriptions that the ambassadors give of the imperial capital share in this vision. The city has not only an obviously privileged strategic position but also a vocation to govern the East and the West, to be the capital of the whole world. In

1503, Andrea Gritti spoke rapturously of the city's beauty: "Its climate, its two seas protecting it on both sides, the beauty of its neighboring lands, give this city what is thought to be the most beautiful and the most favored site not only in all of Asia but in all the world."[111]

One after another, the other ambassadors were struck with this same wonder. Yet sixteenth-century Italy had any number of splendid cities, and the Venetians good reason to be pleased with their own. But Constantinople was unique. Nearly a century after Gritti, Donà echoes his account. Having described the favorable position of Istanbul between Asia and Europe, "the rare beauty, the incalculable advantages" of its site, and every detail of its environs; having acknowledged that the view of the city "is truly the most beautiful thing in the world that there is to see," Donà goes on to say that "that which, above all other conditions, makes [the city] marvelous and truly born for mastery [*imperio*] of a great part of the world, and especially for navigation, is its situation between the channels that I have described, amid the two seas the Turks call the white and the black, which allows a constant coming-and-going of ships conveying every kind of thing from every part of the world."[112]

He then recalls something, not from a book or a manuscript that he had read, but something the senators once told him: that when their forebears controlled part of the city along with the French, they considered moving the whole Republic to that site, "because it was more suitable to their genius for world navigation and for controlling the superb and most fertile neighboring provinces." A peerless city, which in Donà's opinion could still call itself the capital of the world in spite of its having fallen into unworthy hands.

While Donà's extensive description of the city betrays an obsession with the possibility that the Turk might bring about universal monarchy, it also refracts an image that the sultan himself wanted to convey of his position. The series of pairings—two seas, the white and the black, two continents, Europe and

Asia—suggesting mastery of the entire world, are part of the emperor's official epithets. The ambassadors were well acquainted with that preamble to the sultan's missives which rang with proclamation and challenge. The Senate heard it many times, translated into Italian. Here is how Suleiman the Magnificent proclaimed it in 1527, announcing to the doge—"Thou, Andrea, who art doge of Venice"—that ambassador Marco Minio was received at court:

Suleiman, sciach, *filius Selim,* Imperator semper victor; *by god's mercy and the grace of the Prophet Mohammed and by the favor of his four companions and others, I, emperor of emperors, crowned king of men over the whole face of the earth, shadow of god on the two continents, emperor of the White sea and the Black, of Romania and Anatolia, of the countries of Greece and of Caramania, of Dulkadir, Diyarbekir, Dirniazim, Damascus, Aleppo, Cairo, Holy Jerusalem, and of sublime Mecca and revered Medina, of Zide, of Yemen and of many other countries,* Sultan Suleiman, *sciach,* imperator, son of Sultan Selim *sciach,* imperator.[113]

The sultan says it in no uncertain terms: he is master of the two seas and the two continents—the same formula is struck on the imperial currency—and he stands higher than all other men and all the other crowned heads. He is god's shadow on earth. His capital, the Porte, he calls the "seat of felicity." The Venetians also knew that Suleiman had plans to take Rome and that within the Ottoman Empire there had been prophecies already giving him the victory.[114] In these respects the imperial ideology constructs an image that corresponds exactly, like a reflection in a mirror, to the Venetian vision.

(Here Judith sings the aria "rector mundi," master of the world.)

Chorus

Two principal characters, Venice and the Turk; Venice speaks of the Turk. Up until this point, in the 1570s, the political and military institutions of the Ottoman Empire, the men in the sultan's service, had inspired in the Venetians words and ideas of order, beauty, and perfection. To them, the imperial edifice presented a severe and imposing architecture, and its sumptuous grandeur was one they recognized.[115] The abstract categories to which the ambassadors turned to designate the Turkish political regime were those of *governo, dominio, regno, imperio*, neutral and ordinary terms that applied to other European regimes with which the Serenissima maintained relations. Similarly, the official epithets, the honorific qualifiers that accompany the mention of the sultan and his viziers—*magnifico, serenissimo*, and so on—belong to the same family as those bestowed on princes and other notables within the sphere of Christendom. The ambassadors may have emphasized the differences between certain practices of the Ottoman Empire and those of Venice, yet for all of that, the empire was still a legitimate system.

If we were to allow ourselves, for an instant, an immense anachronism, we might say that relations between Venice and the empire were—all things considered—not unlike those between much of the world and the United States in the period since the end of the Second World War. The political, economic, and military hegemony of this new power—this youthful *imperialism*—may be ill abided, but its achievements and its political regime dazzle and fascinate nonetheless. One might wish that it had less power, but no one thinks to challenge its legitimacy.

In Venetian descriptions of the Porte, the term that encompasses the parts of the system as a whole, the locution that summarizes all of its observed qualities, is *imperio*, empire. As indicated in the virtuoso nomenclature of the sultan's honorifics in the various oriental languages which is offered by Erizzo, the final word is that "for us Venetians," all these words mean emperor.[116] A legitimate government, quite obviously. But even more, it is a regime that, for the ambassadors, continues to rank high within the hierarchy of recognized political forms, for it surpasses and coordinates all the others, having itself attained the highest degree of order.

This first conclusion is not entirely self-evident. Quite the contrary, it has been something of a truism that the Ottoman Empire had been perceived, since the sixteenth century and even in Venice, as a barbarous monster, that a stereotype of the absolutist and despotic character of the Ottoman monarchy had been handed down from one century to the next.[117] But as we have seen, it was a very different image that the representatives of the Venetian republic brought back with them from Istanbul. Was theirs an isolated voice? Was it heard? What did the chorus of other authors who wrote about the Turks have to say? It was a vast chorus—so vast, in fact, that it has generally been divided into two groups and assigned to separate areas of the stage.[118] On one side are those authors who restrict their analyses to things Ottoman, who describe the "ways and manners of the Turks" or write about their history; on the other side are those who, whether they draw from the first group or not, graft, as it were, the figure of the Turk onto various branches of European cultural production, from religious debate to fantastic fiction, from court ballet to political philosophy. And for each of those two groups, the practice has been to arrange authors and their works into two columns: Turkophobes and Turkophiles, positive tracts and critical tracts, works that stem from the medieval religious tradition and those prefiguring eighteenth-century philosophy, darkness and light. This double-entry accounting system, organized as a set of two chronologically ordered series of citations, is a convenient classification; it makes it possible to keep the books open, to add an entry to either of the two columns with each discovery of some new *turquerie*.[119] But to proceed thus, extracting citations and aligning them into a paired series, is to risk losing sight of the logic that underlies individual works, or of the particular logic that each author sees at work in the functioning of the Ottoman system.

The Turkish material is a heterogeneous one, and it is best not to pour it into a single mold. For our purposes here, we will isolate a handful of books, those by authors who in their discussions of politics have considered the case of the Turks. There is obviously a polemical intention in this selection, for it calls into question one of political philosophy's standard interpretations. In drawing a straight line from a number of sixteenth-century writers to Montesquieu and then to Marx, political philosophy pulls the earlier writers out of their political and intellectual context in order to make them signposts of a linear history of ideas. Thus Perry Anderson, summarizing a long and remarkable study of the genesis of the notion of the Asiatic mode of production, writes, "Theoretical juxtaposition and contrast of European and Asian state structures formed, as we have seen, a long tradition from Machiavelli and Bodin onwards: prompted by the proximity of Turkish power, it was indeed coeval with the new birth of political theory as such in the Renaissance, and thereafter accompanied its development step by step down to the Enlightenment."[120]

The Venetian ambassadors, we must remember, had read Aristotle and had an intimate knowledge of the Aristotelian vocabulary. They practiced Machiavelli—some of them cite him—and, at the end of the sixteenth century, they would become familiar with the thought of another author, Giovanni Botero. Conversely, the philosophers could read the ambassadorial reports, and the order in which Jean Bodin, for example, presents the characters of the Turkish Empire suggests that he followed the rubrics of the Venetian reports. These texts respond to each other. Let us listen to some of them, beginning with Machiavelli and his frequently invoked chapter four of *The Prince*. Anderson writes that "Machiavelli, in the Italy of the early 16th century, was the first theorist to use the Ottoman State as the antithesis of a European monarchy."[121] It is worthwhile to quote the passage to which he refers:

> [*My answer is that*] *all the principalities we know of have been governed in one of two ways: either by a prince and his servants, who help in the administration of the territory by his grace and favor; or by a prince and by nobles, who hold their rank not by favor of the prince, but by ancient hereditary right. . . .*
>
> *In our own day, examples of these two kinds of government are provided by Turkey and France. The whole Turkish empire is governed by one prince, and all the rest are his servants; the empire is divided up into sandjaks to which he appoints various administrators, whom he transfers or replaces as he likes. But the king of France is surrounded by a multitude of long-established noblemen, who are recognized and beloved by their own subjects; they also have their own hereditary privileges, of which the king cannot deprive them without danger to himself.*[122]

Machiavelli thus underscores a contrast between France and the Ottoman Empire. But does this text alone make him the theorist of an antithesis between European and oriental systems? Can we read into it an unequivocal critique of the Ottoman Empire? In the portion of text that comes between the two paragraphs cited, Machiavelli notes that under the first form of government, the kind personified by the Grand Turk, the prince has more power at his disposal than under the second, for which the model is France. I think I need not point out that for Machiavelli princely power is not a negative value. Pursuing his comparison of the two systems, Machiavelli indicates their contrasting weaknesses. Turkey, he notes, would be a difficult country to conquer but an easy one to hold: once the royal lineage is destroyed, no intermediary body stands in the way of the conquerer. France, on the other hand, would be easy to conquer, because the barons are corruptible, but to maintain possession of it would be difficult, for once the king has been brought down, the nobles would rise up against the usurper. Each system displays compensatory features. The dichotomy that Machiavelli establishes is not black and white; it is more complex than it has generally been made out to be. Most important, it is not the only dichotomy he establishes: his entire argumentation is organized into antithetical pairs. For example, he contrasts two forms of rule—republics and principalities. The principalities are divided in their turn into two categories, the hereditary and the newly acquired, and the latter are then divided into those that are absolutely new and those that are not. Thus the Ottoman Empire belongs to an abstract category, the principality, which stands in opposition to another abstract category, namely, the republic. And within its assigned category, it finds itself in the company of many other countries.

In *The Prince* and in *The Discourses on the First Decade of Livy's History*, the Turks come up repeatedly. Sometimes they illustrate one of Machiavelli's precepts, which are always stated as simple facts. For example, Machiavelli posits that an expanding state can survive the rule of a weak prince, providing his successor is strong. His example is Suleiman, who restored the empire to its former glory after the reign of Bajazet, his feeble predecessor.[123] At other times, the Turks are put in the same category as other peoples and other empires with unambiguously positive connotations, as when they are presented as the inheritors of Roman virtue. In *The Discourses* I, 30, Machiavelli explains that princes who seek to avoid living in constant mistrust should command all their expeditions in person, and he adds, "as the Roman Emperors did in the beginning, and as the

Sultan does at the present time, and as in fact all valiant princes ever have done and will do. For if victorious, all the glory and fruits of their conquests will be theirs."[124]

Finally, in a famous passage in which Machiavelli challenges the thesis that the past is superior to the present, he posits that the sum of good and evil is invariable, that "good and evil change from one country to another." As it moves from place to place, virtue changes hands, passing from one people to another, and the Turks are cited among those who have reclaimed the valor, the virtue, that once belonged to Rome. "The different peoples of these several countries, then, after the fall of the Roman Empire, have possessed and possess still in great part that virtue which is so much lamented and so sincerely praised."[125] And so the Ottoman Empire is accorded a place among the empires marked by excellence, by *virtù*—a union of energy and talent—and is designated, along with "the states of Germany," a successor to the great empires of the past, the Assyrian, the Medean, and the Persian empires, and then Rome. Here, as in the preceding assessments, we see the convergence of Machiavelli's vision with the genealogies drawn by the Venetian ambassadors.

At the same time, Machiavelli—following other authors, or along with them—offers a critique of tyranny. Although there is no need to dwell on this point, we might note that the Turkish Empire does not figure among the examples of tyrannical government with which Machiavelli illustrates his discussion. Here again, the parallels between his analyses and those of the Venetian ambassadors are noteworthy. It is only by having the later categories, particularly that of despotism, already in mind that one could think it possible to find them in Machiavelli; his texts had to be skewed for him to be made the founder of a tradition, the first link in an unbroken chain.

The writings of Jean Bodin have been similarly skewed. Like Machiavelli, Bodin is considered to be one of the ancestors of the notions of oriental despotism and the Asiatic mode of production. He supposedly includes the government of the Ottoman Empire among the forms that despotism could take. "Bodin," writes Perry Anderson, "developed a political contrast between monarchies bound by respect for the persons and goods of their subjects, and empires unrestricted in their dominion over them: the first represented the 'royal' sovereignty of European States, the second the 'lordly' power of despotisms such as the Ottoman State, which were essentially foreign to Europe."[126] Bodin's *Methodus ad facilem historiarum cognitionem* was published for the first time in 1568, *Les six livres de la République* in 1576. To attribute the notion of despotism to their author is, at those dates, still anachronistic. Moreover, it is inaccurate to say that Bodin placed the Ottoman Empire among the abusive and corrupt forms of government. If "royalty turns into tyranny, aristocracy into oligarchy, and democracy into demagogy,"[127] for Bodin, the Turkish Empire has nothing to do with any of these degenerate forms.

We should reread Bodin, not only for the pleasure of commerce with a most stimulating mind, but also and more modestly, in this case, to ascertain what it is he says about the Ottoman Empire. And because having read Machiavelli and Contarini—and Paolo Jovio and Guillaume Postel on the subject of Turkey[128]—he in turn came to be read, discussed, and refuted on the Italian peninsula.

It is in the *Methodus* that Bodin first defines the important notion of sovereignty, according to a schema that he later elaborates in the *République*. The concept is a central one in Bodin, and it is developed through a series of equivalents that one must keep in mind to avoid any possible misunderstanding: supreme authority in which the principle of the commonwealth resides is called "supreme political power" by Aristotle, *signoria* by the Italians (recall that the ambassadors use this word in reference to both Venice and the Ottoman Empire), "supreme authority" or "supreme power" (*summa rerum, summum imperium*) by Latin writers, and *souveraineté*, or "sovereignty," by writers in French. Sovereignty has five attributes by which it can be recognized:

the power to appoint and dismiss the great officers of state, to make and unmake laws, to declare war and sign peace treaties, to be the final resort of appeal from all other courts, and to pardon persons convicted of crimes. Bodin submits that the unanimous opinion of legal scholars recognizes this sovereignty in the prince. In such a case, the government is a monarchy. For Bodin there are three forms of constitution, and only three: government by a single individual, in other words, a monarchy; government by a small number of citizens, which Bodin prefers not to call aristocracy or oligarchy, because these words "introduce considerations of vice and virtue"[129]; and finally, government by the majority of citizens, which Bodin hesitates to call democracy or demagogy, for the same reasons as above. Naturally, the Turkish Empire falls into the category of monarchy, within which Bodin distinguishes between princes who submit to the law and those who are its masters. Turkey, Persia, Scythia, Britain, and Ethiopia belong to this second category. Does Bodin condemn them? Not at all. Let us read what he says: "It is not contrary to nature or to the law of nations that the prince should be master of all things in the state, including its laws, providing he exercises justly the authority that is his by force of arms or by blood: is not the father of a family, by the law of nations, the owner not only of what he earns but also of what his servants earn, nay, of the servants themselves?"[130]

In the first category, Bodin places the princes who conform to the laws, that is, the Christian and North African princes (I must admit that I do not see which Moghrebi ruler he has in mind), and he then concludes that "there is the following difference among the legitimate kings: some are bound by certain laws of the kingdom and others are completely free." *Among the legitimate kings*, he writes. There is no doubt that the prince who holds himself above the law is still a legitimate prince, whether he has come to power through conquest—"by arms"—or through hereditary right—"by blood." When does the prince lose his legitimacy? When the monarchy succumbs to passions and self-interest. Then it degenerates into tyranny, of which

Bodin finds examples both in antiquity and in contemporary Florence.

For Bodin, monarchy is the best form of government. It is in keeping with the laws of nature: "In each part of creation, there is always some one object that excels." The true image of the state can be found in the family. Like the family, the state rests on the authority of a single person, the head of state. Bodin calls upon the Turkish experience:

[*That power belongs to one man*] *Suleiman made plain by a memorable example in the year 1522. When Mustapha, his eldest son, had exhausted the resistance of the Persians and had returned without an escort to his father, trusting to a safe-conduct, he was received with such a clamor by the army, with such favor, as no mortal ever had before. His father could not endure his son's popularity, but ordered him to be strangled in an inner bedroom and then thrown to the army. Thereupon he commanded the herald to proclaim in a loud voice: "There is one God in the heavens; on the earth one man, Suleiman alone, ought to be emperor." The whole army was silent, struck by terror. Two days later a younger son was carried off by poison because he grieved for his brother's death. The third, for fear of his father, fled to the king of the Persians. Immediately he was brought back by envoys and beheaded. There remained only the present Selim, whom his father would have threatened if he had not been the surviving son. This was customary among the race of Ottomans, because the hope of empire will come to all, but attainment to one alone.*[131]

Bodin will return to this theme and to this particular example in the *République*, in which he reaffirms that monarchy is the law of nature and, to illustrate that there can be but one God, one sun, and one king, offers the example of Suleiman and the just punishment of his eldest son. By now, it is perhaps unnecessary to point out the similarity of this analysis to that of the Venetian ambassadors.

But Bodin continues, devoting a chapter to the "refutation of the theory of four monarchies." The arguments he enlists in favor of the Turks are exactly the same and in the same order as those of the Venetian reports: territorial power, abundance of resources, number of men, and, finally, the annexation of the great empires of antiquity:

By what rights does the ruler of Germany compare himself with the sultan of the Turks? Who could be more aptly called a monarch than the latter? This fact is obvious to everyone—if anywhere there exists an authority worthy of the name of empire or of authentic monarchy, it is surely the sultan who wields it. He occupies the richest lands of Asia, Africa, and Europe; his dominion extends throughout the Mediterranean, with the exception of a few islands. His military might rivals that of all the other princes combined: he has driven the Persian and the Muscovite troops far beyond his borders, he has conquered Christian kingdoms and the Byzantine empire and has even laid waste the German provinces. . . .

It would be far more just to regard the Osmanli sultan as the inheritor of the Roman Empire, for it was he who, after capturing the imperial capital of Byzantium from the Christians, went on to conquer from the Persians that region of Babylonia which is spoken of in the Book of Daniel, adding to the ancient provinces of Rome all the land across the Danube until the banks of the Borysthenes, which now constitutes the greatest part of his territory.

As he had for Machiavelli, the Turk now occupies the place that once belonged to Rome. He has surpassed the empires of the past and can now claim his inheritance:

Whether we define monarchy by the might of its army, the extent of its resources, the fertility of its territory, the roster of its victories, the number of its inhabitants, or, considering only the etymology of the term, by the fact that it applies to Daniel's fatherland or to the emperor of Babylon, we must recognize that the prophecy of Daniel can be most appropriately interpreted as applying to the sultan of the Turks.[132]

Bodin ultimately rejects the translation of Daniel's prophecy into secular political philosophy and concludes that today "all men share a common bond and participate marvelously in the universal commonwealth, as though they formed a single city." Notwithstanding, his text conveys the same visions that can be glimpsed in the Venetian reports.

In the *République*, Bodin further refines his typology of governments. He distinguishes three forms of monarchy: royal monarchy, under which all the subjects obey the king; tyrannical monarchy, under which the king, rejecting the laws of nature and of men, abuses people and their property alike; and last, "seignorial monarchy," *la monarchie seigneuriale.* Is the Ottoman Empire of the second type? Does the sultan trample on people and things? No. Here again, he falls into the category of "seignorial monarchs." He is not a tyrant, for tyranny presupposes usurpation and the sultan has won his empire in just wars.[133]

As a "seignorial monarchy," the Ottoman Empire belongs to the same category as Muscovy. The sultan of Turkey is an absolute sovereign like the kings of France, Spain, England, Scotland, Persia, and Ethiopia. It is unlawful for subjects to make any attempt against the honor, life, or dignity of such rulers. Not once does the Ottoman Empire appear as an example of a monarchy that has succumbed to tyranny. Neither in Bodin's nor in Machiavelli's taxonomies does the empire figure among illegitimate or degenerate governmental forms.

Etienne de La Boétie, another reputed forefather of Montesquieu's oriental despotism, is the last author we will consider here. His work was not published within his own lifetime; his *Discours de la servitude volontaire* first circulated as a manuscript. After La Boétie's death in 1563, Montaigne, who was his friend, published his entire oeuvre with the exception of the *Discours.* That text was brought out by Calvinists in a pirated edition in 1574 and enjoyed wide popularity before falling into two centuries of oblivion. Tyranny is, of course, one of the central themes of this work. La Boétie exposes its three forms and lists the methods that tyrants use to remain in power. Remarkably, he draws all his examples from antiquity, except in one case, in which we find at last the Turkish Empire. One of the means by which tyrants stay in power, he writes, is to keep men apart from one another, prevent them from assembling, from speaking and writing to one another. They turn their subjects into senseless beasts. And the sultan of Turkey, says La Boétie, even with very few wise men in his land and no books there at all, has understood this perfectly.[134] La Boétie subscribes principally to the idea that people have "natures" that should be nourished and thereby, like plants, be improved upon. And going back to the commonly held myth about Venice, the state of liberty, he contrasts the condition of the Venetian citizens to the brutalization that prevailed in the states of the Grand Signor. The words "tyrant" and "tyranny" are not yet spoken in connection with the Turk, but the contrast in the human condition under various systems is nowhere as marked as in this text:

> *Anyone who saw the Venetians, a tiny nation living in such liberty that the worst rogue among them would not wish to be their king, born and bred with a single avowed ambition to excel their fellows in meticulous and vigilant care to uphold liberty, formed from the cradle to reject all other worldly goods rather than lose one iota of their freedom—anyone, I say, who saw those people and then went to the realm of the man we call the Grand Signor, and saw how people there reckon that the sole purpose of their existence is to serve this man and to sacrifice their lives to keep him in power: would he reckon that these two nations shared a common nature, or would he not rather judge that he had left a city and entered a sheepfold?*[135]

Like Judith, Venice is the embodiment of liberty, and the Turk, like Holofernes, is now the "impious tyrant."

PART TWO

"Greater tyranny the world has never seen or imagined"

At the twilight of the sixteenth century, the image that the Venetian ambassadors give of the Ottoman Empire clouds over, the sovereign's portrait takes on a grimace, and cracks begin to appear in every part of the imperial edifice.[136] Territorially, of course, the Ottoman Empire was still the most extensive in the world, and with new conquests at Persia's expense, it grew vaster still. It remained, without a doubt, the most redoubtable and most important consideration of the Venetian strategy, and the ambassadors' reports continue to dwell on such themes as its inexhaustible human and material resources, the exceptionally favorable situation of its capital, the proven qualities of its army, and the progress it still showed itself to be capable of. Some ambassadors find formulas even more resounding than those of their predecessors at the beginning of the century. "Rome," exclaims one of them, "is the epitome of the world, but Constantinople is the world of the world." Another proclaims that "the Turk has reached the gates of our Italy, garden of the world and center of Christendom" and now aspires "to universal monarchy." Agostino Nani put it in a way that would have pleased Fernand Braudel. This empire, he says, "is more a world than a state."[137]

Yet, at the same time, the Venetian ambassadors describe a process of corruption, of decomposition affecting the system in each of its parts. Whereas in the writings of the earlier ambassadors the word *ordine*—referring sometimes to the power of the sovereign, sometimes to the perfect organization of the civil and military corps—came up again and again, now, with the century drawing to a close, expressions of the empire's dysfunction begin to accumulate. In a copious report whose wide circulation and considerable fame suggest that we pause for a moment to consider it more closely, Lorenzo Bernardo writes: "Al presente tutto questo ordine si va alterando e corropendo."— "Today that order is all being changed and corrupted." The janissaries, he continues, in their entire history never knew defeat, yet today they are *cascati*, they have tumbled from their former valor. The Ottoman fleet, though still feared by all the princes of the world, is now "diminished" in number, in experience, and in quality, and, moreover, its men are poorly paid. Above all, he writes, the "three foundations" on which the Turks had built up their power in so little time—religion, obedience, and parsimony, which we should take to mean the art of living and governing at the least expense, the careful management of resources—have been shaken. The Turks have lost their religious unity, their warlike ardor, and their virile frugality. "Disunity" and "disobedience" have found their way into the civil and military corps. Bernardo does not yet speak of an irreversible decline, and he reminds his readers emphatically that this empire "has never lost a single span of conquered territory" and that it may yet maintain some of its momentum. But he detects several "principles of decline," among the most salient of which is the transformation of the victorious prince into a man of the palace, the degeneration of the triumphant empire into a passive machine.

Underlying Bernardo's entire analysis is a reference to the Roman model and the idea that empires, like living beings, have their youth, their maturity, and their decline. As in Rome after the Trajans, a succession of indolent rulers has squandered the glory won by their triumphant predecessors.[138] Later reports do more than announce the empire's decline; they describe it and analyze its causes. It is seen, by turns, as a consequence of a war against Persia which proved too costly, as the result of the influence of women over the prince, as a symptom of weak leadership.[139] But more important, perhaps, is the fact that from now on the Ottoman Empire belongs to a different horizon. All of the reports emphasize the empire's fundamental incompatibility with the Venetian system; and for several ambassadors, the starting point of their reports, their basic premise, is that the two orders are absolutely at variance with each other.[140] The reports from the early part of the sixteenth century all compare implicitly or explicitly the Ottoman institutions with those of Venice or, more generally, with those of Christendom, and on many points the Turks compare favorably. The relationship is reversed after 1575, even if certain Turkish practices are still held forth as examples for the Christian world.[141] The appraisal of the Turks now takes place under the sign of negation, lack, shortcoming, and loss. Morosini tells us that the sultan has very *little* courage, his first vizier a very *short* memory; the third vizier is a man of *little* judgment; the second is remarkable, but the others think *little* of him because he has no experience in war and is believed to have *little* courage.[142] The sultan, he writes, lacks good counselors and able commanders—but not arrogant ones. The Turks lack civility in their social relations, in their table manners, their architecture, and their urban planning; they lack expertise in the arts and in technologies; they lack the knowledge for speculative activities.[143] They are base, abject, ignoble, boorish, ignorant, barbarous, villainous, proud, insolent, inhumane, bereft of faith, trust, and honor: all of these predicates now rain down upon the Turks. "In every one of their customs," Morosini continues, "they do exactly the contrary of what Christians do, and one would think that this is precisely what their legislator intended when he decreed their ceremonies. . . . In every one of their actions, they do the opposite of what we do. Few Turks are adept at operating machinery; they do not cultivate the land, and they have no other occupations to speak of; they take no delight in virtue of any sort, play neither handball nor football, do not

train horses, do not fire cannon balls; their only pastime is archery."[144]

Their sherbets are not "to Italian tastes," writes one ambassador, adding that they use neither knives, nor forks, nor nap-
kins, even at court banquets. Another, referring to the fifty
dishes set down before the sultan at meals, comments that "they
would give us nausea, not pleasure."[145] The Turks are thus as
inept at leisure as they are at work, are mediocre both in the
occupations of daily life and in the luxuries of the court.

The painstaking and circumspect descriptions from the beginning of the century now give way to negative discourses. But
the better arguments, which is to say those more likely to have
an effect on their audience, are those structured around the opposition between what reason dictates—what Venice's reason
dictates, needless to say—and what the Turks do: it is not to
several men that the Grand Signor entrusts the government of so
great an empire but to one man alone; the vizier owes his power
not to his virtue or merit but to the sovereign's caprices. In
other countries justice and reason have their due place; here, the
will commands, guided by passion. When administering justice,
the Turks do not rely on legal writings but decide their verdicts
on the basis of oral testimony alone.[146] The rhetoric of denunciation has supplanted that of observation. Nothing is spared. To
criticisms of social practices and complaints about the sultan's
officers are added indictments against his religion—now described as a false and accursed religion that causes moral deprav-
ity and subverts human relations. The signs are all inverted
now. Arguments that a short time ago were offered in favor of
Turkish superiority are now invoked to impugn the Ottoman
order. Reading about the great deeds of the heroes of old used to
inspire the deeds of the conquering sultans; now it fuels their
madness by making them believe in a greatness they cannot attain. Respect for religious law used to guarantee justice in government; now it is a false law and contributes toward making
the government monstrous. Promotions based on training re-

ceived in the seraglio and on demonstrated merit used to offer every man the opportunity to serve the emperor by giving the best of himself; the Venetian ambassador now discovers that, to the contrary, the "magnificent" vizier is simply a "rogue in disguise."[147] The sultan's power is no longer a blinding fact to which the ambassadors submit. Even as they continue to describe its every aspect, they now see it as an illusion that he both harbors and is caught up in; it is like the obverse of a medallion whose real value can be read by turning it over. "Arrogant foolishness," immoderation, a pride that is "fuor di modo"—beyond decency—place the monarch, his familiars, and the empire outside the limits of rationality.

It is in form and style of government and in sociopolitical order that the opposition between Venice and Christendom, on the one hand, and the Ottoman Empire, on the other, is the most radical. On one side, a free population, a hereditary aristocracy, and stable, lawful institutions. On the other side, the eradication of the nobility in every conquered country and the reduction of all subjects to servitude such that the entire social body is brought down to a common level of utter indignity.[148] The empire "is a government or republic of slaves."[149] Hoisted into power on the whims of the monarch, such men can only be dishonest and untrustworthy, for a slave under any circumstances is low and servile. Finally—and this is another factor making the decline of the Ottomans inevitable—when the expansion of an empire begins to slow, its preservation depends on the quality of its institutions; when the fruits of conquest have been spent, the benefits of just government must take their place. The Ottoman Empire has failed to carry out this conversion.

There was a name for bad government of this sort; it was called tyranny. Applied to every level of the Ottoman reality, the word now appears in its verbal and nominal as well as adjectival forms and in association with other concepts that intensify its meaning. "Their proper state is tyranny, violence, and usurpation":[150] in point of fact, the notion of tyranny already implies usurpation in the first place. The Ottoman government is therefore not legitimate, for it is a government obtained by force, not by inheritance or by the consent of a free population.[151] Taken by force, power is maintained through the use of force. Relations between the ruler and his subjects are characterized by violence rather than by common reference to a body of laws and legal institutions. Such power is thus the power of insanity, the *irragionavole governo*,[152] whose excesses find expression in the persistent practice of arbitrary seizures of men, goods, and money. "Extortion" is the natural means of tyrannical government, "oppression" the natural condition of its subjects. Tyranny is the kingdom of fear; the ambassadors call it by its various names (*paura, spavento, timore*) and describe it in all its effects. Every member of the social body is fear-stricken. Subjects are caught in the grip of fear because the sultan is the master of their property and their lives. His viziers are afraid too, for those who have risen highest have reason to fear the most brutal fall. At the slightest incident, the sultan can "remove" their heads. But if he "causes trembling" in everyone around him, he too is ruled by suspicion and fear, for he can trust no one. Being government by extremity, tyranny rests on an absurd logic: first it destroys the nobility to hoist into power men who have emerged from the rabble, and then it proceeds to destroy the countries and populations that feed it. The king cannot increase his levies, as is the practice in the Christian lands, because since all his subjects are slaves, he has no one left on whom to impose new taxes.[153] Montesquieu will give this observation the force of law: "In despotic states, [taxes] cannot be increased, because one cannot increase the extremity of servitude."[154] Having devoured its subjugated peoples, tyranny ultimately devours itself. A sea swallowing up the rivers that pour into it, a chain of thieves each of whom steals from those below what is then stolen from him by those above:[155] the ambassadors have any number of metaphors to describe the progress of violence and death. The oppressed subjects of tyranny are "eaten to the bone"; the countries it acquires are depopulated; the earthly paradises that fall into its hands become deserts, and wherever its power goes, death goes too. All of these things define tyranny.

In a system such as this, the prince "knows no other reason than his own will,"[156] for, having grown up apart from the world, a prisoner of the seraglio, he is neither disciplined nor wise.[157] Nor does he have wise men to counsel him, because he has eradicated the nobility; even his own slaves can no longer advise him, because the sultan prefers the company of subhumans—women, dwarfs, and mutes—to that of men.[158] Though he has absolute power—*il assoluto dominio*—the tyrant in fact surrenders it to the grand vizier, a man chosen not for his own virtue but rather by some caprice on the part of the sultan.[159] Also, the emperor has "no other ear" than that of the vizier with which to hear the noises of the empire, "no other mouth" with which to decide, order, dispense, and condemn, "no other head" to administer that vast domain. Master of an illegitimate state, the tyrant cedes his power to an illegitimate minister. Thus reduced to the will of a single man, power can only turn violent and arbitrary.[160] Again in accordance with an absurd logic, not only can the tyrant order his subjects killed, not only can he make them go willingly to their deaths, he can also destroy his own blood.[161] The empire operates from top to bottom as a tremendous killing machine.

The word "tyranny" already appears in certain Venetian reports prior to 1575. The first occurrence is in Navagero's text of 1553, which makes two references to the sultan's tyrannical officers. Twenty years later, Garzoni speaks specifically of the tyranny that Turks of all social circumstances exert against the Christians, while Barbaro speaks of provinces "tyrannized" and countries destroyed.[162] In a formulation that could easily pass for one of Montesquieu's, Barbaro writes that "subornation, violence, and tyranny are natural conditions." But the reports from this period in which such notations occur are relatively few and far between, as are the specific notations themselves within those texts. They denounce the practices of the periphery, not those of the center—it is the sultan's agents who persecute the Christians. They condemn abuses of the system rather than the system itself. After 1575, however, it is the entire edifice that perpetrates the greatest tyranny in history.

Cristoforo Valier's report of 1616 is the last in its series. Those that came immediately after it have been lost, and we must await the return of Giovanni Cappello in 1634 for a new picture of the situation in the Turkish Empire. In the final series of reports which begins with Cappello's, the notion of tyranny continues to characterize the system as a whole,[163] much as it did in the reports from the end of the sixteenth century and the beginning of the seventeenth. The monstrous nature of this form of government is accentuated further and is celebrated in those royal portraits such as that of Murad IV with which this book opened. Words that in the sixteenth century had a neutral meaning and simply referred to strong government now come to signify an abusive, excessive, and degenerate governmental form. In 1616 Valier already contrasts *dominio* with "principality" or "empire." This empire, he writes, "might more properly be called *dominio* than principality or empire."[164] From now on, *dominio* will connote domination rather than dominion. Similarly *assoluto*, already in frequent use in the sixteenth century, now combines with *dominio* and *autorità* to stigmatize abusive government.

A new word—*monarco*—comes to be used to refer to the prince. Prince, sultan, Grand Turk, Grand Signor, all these terms remain in use. But "monarch," more abstract, refers to a specific type of government and stresses the concentration of power in the hands of a single master.

And suddenly there emerges a new tool with which to characterize the Grand Turk's regime: it is now despotic. The word had made a tentative appearance in an anonymous report to which Albèri has difficulty assigning a date—1579 perhaps, or possibly 1582. The term appears parenthetically, in its adjectival form *dispotico* and with no further comment.[165] Then it disappears for a good half-century. After 1634 its career is under way: the adjective will be used regularly in conjunction with the nouns *governo, dominio,* and *autorità*. A few texts introduce the verb *despotizzare*. But the invention of the abstact category of despotism will not occur until the end of the seventeenth century. Moreover, "despotic" does not supplant words that had been coined around the notion of tyranny. Instead, the words "tyrannical" and "despotic" carry each other along, synonymous and interchangeable, and pursue a common career throughout the rest of the century.

At the Sublime Porte

What accounts for this rupture in the Venetian discourse about the Grand Turk? By what metamorphosis did the mighty body of the Ottoman colossus change into an ailing monster? What could turn an emperor who aspired to universal monarchy and seemed capable of attaining it into an unworthy ruler, a tyrant, a despot? Did the changes take place at the "objective" level, in the Turkish polity itself, or rather in the image that the Venetians perceived, the one they constructed? What had changed? The Grand Turk's pose, the pictorial technique, or the painter himself? Or was it perhaps the relation between the painter and his model? By formulating these questions, I am already indicating several possible viewing angles or, rather, have drawn three ellipses whose centers are occupied alternately by the Sublime Porte and by Venice.

At the Sublime Porte: yes, things were going badly, or at least not as well as before. Recent historiography has confirmed some of the symptoms observed by the Venetian ambassadors, has discovered others, and uses the term "decline" in speaking of the totality of processes that affected the empire. One reads, for example, of the high cost of the campaigns against Persia for diminished revenues and fewer territorial gains. Between 1578 and 1590 the empire had conquered large parts of the Caucasus, Kurdistan, and Azerbaijan and then lost them in 1603–1604. There were high costs, too, especially political ones, in the continuing conflicts with the Hapsburgs between 1593 and 1606: with the signing of the peace treaty, the sultan managed to maintain his suzerainty over the Danube principalities, but he had lost many men and, in a historically unprecedented concession, agreed to treat the Hapsburg emperor as an equal, no longer exacting regular tribute from him in exchange for his control of northern Hungary. The administration was corrupt from top to bottom. In a system whose linchpin was the sultan himself, any weakening at the center affected the entire structure. Now, the sultans at this critical period are said to have lacked the qualities of their predecessors. Raised not on the battlefield but in the harem, and without the benefit of having governed the provinces before coming to power, they were incapable of leadership and were helpless before the insubordination and insolence of the janissaries. Murad III (1574–1595) had his five brothers killed on the day of his accession; he had about forty concubines who gave him some one hundred thirty sons and no one knows how many daughters. When his successor, Mehemet III (1595–1603), came to power, he had nineteen of his brothers and more than twenty sisters killed, and over the course of his reign four of his sons would meet the same fate. When these sultans stopped eliminating their rivals physically, there was nothing to prevent the formation of contending factions within the seraglio or the deleterious influence of wives and mothers, the famous sultanate of women.[166] Events such as these should not be discounted in a system in which politics coordinated and integrated the various parts of a vast empire and the activities of its inhabitants.[167]

Beneath the stratum of political personnel and politico-military institutions, other changes have been observed that might seem to have made the decline of the empire an irreversible one. These changes come at the same time as the shift in perspective we have seen in the reports of Venetian ambassadors. There was the demographic growth of the sixteenth century, resulting in general overpopulation and a rural exodus. The overcrowded cities were mobbed with students, restless and defiant, ready to join in the endemic uprisings.

There was also a price revolution in Europe, set off by the Great Discoveries and the Atlantic trade, and its waves reached all the way to the Ottoman empire. But here, inflation did not stimulate the economy; rather, it hurt those social classes that lived on their rents or on fixed salaries. Some people managed to offset the decline in their incomes by selling themselves to the highest bidder, which encouraged widespread corruption, while others shirked their obligations to the state and turned their *timars*, the tax farms they were given to administer, into huge private estates that they exploited for personal benefit. It was a vicious circle: when the state, a victim itself of the rise in prices, no longer received its expected revenues, it turned to monetary manipulation and grew ever more dependent on bribery, extortions, requisitions, and seizures. At the same time, rising European demand for such raw materials as wheat, wool, and metals strained both local consumers and the urban trades.

This line of argumentation raises questions that further research may eventually resolve or recast. If there was a population increase, could it not have been a growth factor, a spur to intensified development? There was certainly no shortage of space, and under such conditions, population growth is supposed to promise increased revenues for producers. If janissaries and spahis shirked their duties, entered civil life, and became merchants and tradesmen, might not this shift have provided a salutary push to the urban economy? Is it not perhaps an indication that the guild system was not as hermetically closed as it has been described to us? And finally, if the health of the empire no longer rested on conquest and on military organization, why did this transformation necessarily result in a decline? Was the emperor's tyranny somehow foreordained?

At all events, within the wheels of empire, things were moving. Things, and also men and ideas. The subjects were aware of the changes taking place and reacted to them in a number of ways. There were collective reactions: the year 1591–1592, corresponding to the year 1000 of the Hegira, brought millenary expectations, swelling fears of and hopes for a liberating crisis.[168] Another collective reaction, this one violent, was the revolt that broke out in Anatolia in 1596, following the imposition of measures aimed at restoring discipline in the army; the insurrection spread to other sectors, set Istanbul aflame, and sprang up again in Anatolia several times before being crushed in 1608. And finally, there was the intellectual reaction, which concerns us more directly here: Ottoman contemporaries analyzed the empire's troubles and in their search for remedies turned to history and to reformulations of political ethics. The Ottomans had their Machiavellis and their Ibn Khalduns, their intellectual innovators and politicians—some out of favor, some not—who knew themselves capable of advising their prince. What did they have to say?

They all refer to the Circle of Equity, which summarizes the essentials of Ottoman political philosophy. Ascribed to Aristotle, the Circle of Equity was actually formulated by the Persian Jalal al-Din Davani, who died at the beginning of the sixteenth century, and was then taken up by Ottoman thinkers, who produced a number of variants. The Circle of Equity set forth the principles of good government in the following terms: sovereign power cannot exist without an army; for there to be an army, there must be wealth; for there to be wealth, there must be subjects; subjects are loyal only if there is justice, which there cannot be without harmony on earth; there can be no harmony on earth without a state; no state without law; and no support for that law without a sovereign power.[169]

The important thing to note here is that justice based on law is presented as the counterweight to the sovereign's absolute power. Law meant not only *shari'a*, religious law, universal and immutable, but also *kanûn*, the dynastic legislation introduced by the great sultans. Indeed, for Ottoman thinkers, the principal legacy of the great rulers of the past was the body of legislation they created. The historian Mustafa Ali (1541–1600), who wrote during the troubled period at the end of the sixteenth century, thought that the fundamental importance of the reign of Mehemet the Conqueror lay in the fact that he had established a law, *kanûn*, to consolidate his empire. The empire would be destroyed, this historian wrote, either when people ceased to obey the law—"when our descendants will say that *kanûn* is what they decide," when human caprices become more important than respect for a law that all share and recognize—or when the ranks of the army were penetrated by foreigners.

Similarly, Suleiman is known as the Legislator, *Kanûnî*, the man who gave his expanding empire stable institutions. Kinalizade Ali Celebi (d. 1572) credits him with having founded "the virtuous city," *medine-i fazili*, and with having given the empire its institutional form by reconciling *shari'a* and *kanûn*.

Mustafa Ali, who had served in the imperial administration, drew on his political experience in writing his *Nushat üs-salâtin* (Counsel for sultans) in 1581. He dedicates the work to Murad III, and in it he lists the disorders from which the empire was suffering—arbitrary authority, corruption, and institutional ineffectiveness. He sees the history of the Moslem states as a cyclical series of expansions, declines, and falls. Corruption, venality, debauchery on the part of the ruler, the influence of women on government, and plague are the signs of decline, and their appearance signifies that the ruler has become a tyrant and thus that the dynasty is liable to be overthrown. The bulwark against such decadence is justice and order, based on law. In his *Seasons of Sovereignty* (1598), the historian sets forth the general principles of a state's legitimacy using examples from the dynasties of Islam's classical period: a just government is one that is based on authority rather than on dynasty or conquest; adherence to the law in both of its forms, *shari'a* and *kanûn*, is what makes lasting dynasties possible. How can the decline of the state be checked? By returning to the past—its great sultans and their ways. By putting an end to monetary manipulations that disrupt equitable exchange and make a policy of fair prices impossible, for accord-

ing to Mustafa Ali, it is the duty of the central power to regulate
the social distribution of wealth. It is also its duty to set the
pillars of the imperial administration aright by maintaining the
principle of promotion according to merit and by drawing on
the empire's resources to train, within the palace itself, compe-
tent officials devoted to the emperor.[170]

Political ethics and unease about the present state of the empire also found expression in verse. In a doleful poem written
about 1581–1582, Mustafa Ali speaks of the poison that the cup
of destiny held in store for every member of the social body,
from the sultan to his vizier, from the ulemas to the governors
and merchants. Another learned poet, writing in 1608, dreams
of a conversation between Alexander the Great and Ahmed I,
the reigning emperor, in which "a tyranny worse than that of
the pharoah" is menaced with the last judgment: the word of
God is no longer respected; the *cadis* are corrupt; the *timars* are
dispensed among the favorites; women and minions are in control of the government; the janissaries are in revolt; and the state
functionaries are all depraved and tyrannical.[171]

Finally, there is the famous epistle, or *Risala*, by Koshu Bey,
an Ottoman official who has been regarded as a kind of Turkish
Montesquieu. He composed his tract in 1630, during the reign
of Murad IV, whom he had served as a close adviser. In nineteen
chapters, he criticizes the present state of the empire, explains
the causes of its enfeeblement, and calls for the restoration of
imperial order. Military organization is disintegrating, with the
destruction of the system of *timars* and the swelling of the jan-
nissary corps with incompetent recruits. The treasury is emptying in spite of the exorbitant increases in taxes, and state revenues are being spent as fast as they come in. Civil and judicial
offices are sold to the highest bidder, and because those who
obtain them cannot be certain of keeping them, they are given to
arbitrary practices. The people have lost their respect for their
judges. The corruption rampant within the imperial household
has now spread to the entire social body. And at the root of it all

is the crisis at the center, where the decisions are made. The sultan no longer looks after the direction of the state, and ever since Suleiman the Magnificent ushered in a reign of favorites by entrusting the post to Ibrahim Pasha rather than to a man of proven political abilities, the offices of the vizier have been debased as well. That double failure has led to the rise of a pack of eunuchs, women, and non-Moslems who now rule the palace. It is urgent that the sultan restore order.

Oppression, injustice, extortion, corruption, and tyranny: all these evils are denounced by the Ottoman authors; those are their words. The agreement between their analyses and that of the Venetian ambassadors is striking indeed. The Turkish writers, of course, remain with their eyes turned to the past and find their points of reference in the forms and models of the Islamic tradition, be they Arab, Persian, or Turkish. The format they follow is that of *The Mirror for Princes*, a didactic genre intended for rulers and their courts, and they are faithful to the themes and the structures that the genre entailed. They hold to the model of the Circle of Equity, to the leitmotif of a golden age that lay in the Ottoman dynasty's past. Given their reliance on precedents, it is not surprising that they see salvation for the empire in the restoration of Islam and the traditions of the earlier sultans, in a return to strong and direct royal rule. But the principal aspects of the malaise afflicting the empire at the end of the sixteenth century and in the first third of the seventeenth are indeed those that are noted by the Serenissima's ambassadors.

Seen from Venice, the evolution of the empire would appear to follow from a familiar theoretical model: the decadent form of monarchy being tyranny, the Ottoman Empire illustrated the degeneration of a legitimate form of government. And the Venetian ambassadors would thus have grasped the process even as it was taking place. But something is at odds with that account. Formerly, when the Grand Signor was ordering the murder of his sons and brothers, when he was striking terror in all his subjects, when his blinding presence made it impossible to behold him face to face, he nonetheless belonged to the family of legitimate monarchs. When he alone wielded his power and his mere gestures could command, he was not called a tyrant, though everyone knew what a tyrant was. Consider by contrast Ahmed I, who came to power in 1603. He brought the practice of fratricide to a halt. He was a poet and a pious man. He built mosques and schools, reestablished respect for religious norms. In Venice, however, they spoke of his government as tyrannical. If the discourse had shifted, it was because something quite apart from the very real "data" of the Turkish world must have weighed in the balance.

It was not Lepanto. The victory of the Holy League did not fundamentally alter the correlation of forces between Christians and Turks. The Christians won. They destroyed the Ottoman fleet, killed thirty thousand of the enemy and took three thousand prisoner. The victory celebrations mobilized the church and the people, poets and painters, composers and popular singers. In Venice, as soon as the victory was announced, the Council of Ten decided to commission one or several painters to immortalize the battle. Tintoretto set to work, as did Vasari in Rome. Titian painted for Philip II. Others would follow.[172] Returning to the formula Minio had used at the beginning of the century, Maffeo Venier states in the report he presented in 1586 that now was the time to launch a Christian offensive "that will penetrate to the entrails of the Turkish state."[173] But Venice had come away from the confrontation exhausted, and despite what it had agreed to at the formation of the League, it abandoned the struggle and was first to make a separate peace with the enemy; Venice accepted the loss of Cyprus and an increase in the annual tribute it paid to the emperor in exchange for the renewal of its commercial privileges. Its good relations with the empire lasted until the end of the reign of Murad IV.[174]

As for the other partners, after Lepanto they brought their anti-Ottoman offensive to a halt. The Christian fleet withdrew to the western Mediterranean and left the Turk in control over the eastern Mediterranean. Within several months, he had recovered his strength. The Turkish fleet again attacked Sicily and southern Italy in 1574. Having consolidated his hold on North Africa with the capture of Tunis in 1574, the Turk would now turn his efforts against Persia on one flank and against the Hapsburgs on the other.

The reversal of the power relation between Europe and the Ottoman Empire took place over the long term. Individually, none of the European states could prevail against the Turk. Furthermore, during the period in which we see the image of the Grand Signor wavering, each of those states found itself grappling with new difficulties: Venice had an inexorable commercial and economic decline to contend with, and then twenty-four years of latent or active war with the Turks, between 1645 and 1669, which resulted in the loss of Crete, a Venetian possession since the thirteenth century; Spain had the disaster of the Invincible Armada in 1588; for the Hapsburg Empire there was the Thirty Years' War (1618–1648). There is no need, after those superb pages that Fernand Braudel has devoted to Lepanto, to go back over the ramifications of this event, nor should we inflate any sentiments of military or naval superiority that the Christian powers might have felt with regard to the Turk. And so we must shift our viewing angle once again, station ourselves in Venice, and from Venice turn our gaze to Europe itself.

The Abduction
from the Seraglio

In Europe, the dream of a Christian commonwealth was growing more remote, the illusion of political unity was fading, and the nation-states were on the rise. The project of universal monarchy was losing ground to the reality of local but absolutist monarchies. With mutations in political consciousness in the various parts of Europe, with religious disputes, civil wars, and revolutions, came an effervescence in political literature.

The history of these upheavals cannot be told here; we will simply indicate its principal markers. The Serenissima, for its part, was seeking to define a new identity for itself in the final third of the seventeenth century. The political elite feared a decline of the Republic's institutions. It watched the changes taking place in Florence under the Medicis. It saw Venice's independence threatened by Spain and Rome. With the Holy See, the crisis that had begun in the 1580s culminated in 1606 when the pope put all the territories belonging to the Republic under interdict and at the same time excommunicated the Senate. The time had come to reshuffle the deck, to redefine Venice's political values with respect to the rest of the Italian peninsula and Europe. In this context, the victory at Lepanto, for which the Venetians took full credit, certainly played a role: it allowed for a greater sense of security on the part of the Venetian patriciate, a more vigorous and more dynamic reaffirmation of Venetian republicanism, an open denunciation of what the Republic could not permit itself to become.[175]

At first, Florence was the anti-Venice. In their reports from that city, the ambassadors present the Florentine model as one in which men are governed not by laws but by other men. Florence is tyranny incarnate. In Florence everything depends on the will of a single man; the government is secret; neighbor spies on neighbor; the inhabitants are demoralized and are no longer free. A report by Vicenzo Fedeli, in 1561, accuses the prince of keeping his subjects enslaved. Lorenzo Priuli, in a 1566 report, describes the Florentine prince as the tyrant of three republics, to whom even the word "liberty," that sacred noun, is abhorrent. With the death of his wife, he begins to dishonor the wives of his subjects while availing himself of their wealth. Father and son are both immersed in the love of women. Excessive democracy has made the bed that tyrannical government now lies on. The Medicis are again taken to task in 1588, by Tomaso Contarini: they bought the popular suffrage in order to dominate; they grant favors to their partisans and use fear and intimidation to govern everyone else. The Medicis have relied on the support of the populace to bring down the nobility. Florence, free city, has been humbled. The themes are familiar ones: together, these traits form the outlines of the anti-Venice in its Florentine version, the counterpart of the Turkish version drawn by the ambassadors to the Porte.[176]

Venice's ambassadors to England, after the reestablishment of normal relations with this country, took home similar images. Nicolo Molin, ambassador to James I, speaks of the government's tyrannical beginnings and describes the king as being the absolute master in all things, even though he was assisted by counselors. With the outbreak of the Revolution, Ambassador Giovanni Sagredo discusses Cromwell in terms that we have seen applied to the Grand Turk: he seized power forcibly and now holds his people in servitude. He is more feared than loved and is haunted by suspicion. Sagredo, in 1656, concludes that the government will not last, but he does not call it tyrannical or despotic. Several years later, in analyzing the crisis from which

England had emerged, Angelo Correr and Michele Morosini include Charles I's tendency to absolutism among the factors that led to his fall, and they denounce Cromwell's tyrannical rule.[177]

These signs are all in agreement: first, the Ottoman Empire did not have a monopoly on absolutist or tyrannical government. The family of tyrants counted European rulers among its members. At the same time, tyranny ceased to be a model that belonged to antiquity; its embodiments could be found, *hic et nunc*, within the political horizon of the late-sixteenth and the seventeenth centuries. It was therefore against that model, and against any other threat to Venetian independence—Counter-Reformation culture, the consolidation of monarchical regimes—that Venice, though an oligarchy itself, shored up its libertarian and republican convictions. And against the old guard as well: the political crisis that erupted in 1582 pitted traditionalists against reformers. The reformers, the Giovani, prevailed and over the next thirty years imparted a new style of government to their republic. The reversal that we have seen in the depictions brought back from Istanbul was thus coeval with this reassertion of Venetian political consciousness, with its vigilant distrust of monarchies that could at any moment descend into tyranny.

At Venice's borders and elsewhere in Europe, arguments about good government were raging, and religious conflicts were tearing at the social fabric. The Turk figured in each of these confrontations: during the Wars of Religion in France there were reciprocal accusations of "Calvinoturkism" and "Turkopapism"; following the Saint Bartholomew's Day Massacre the French monarchy was suspected of wanting to "reduce the kingdom to a state of Turkish-like tyranny." It became standard practice to invoke the example of Turkey at any mention of tyranny. But as these vast debates go beyond the scope of our discussion, we cannot dwell on them here.[178] We will, however, pause one last time on a point of historical semantics.

At the beginning of this book, I indicated the central place of Aristotle in the program of studies at the Paduan academies and in Venetian political thought in general. Aristotle had inscribed within Greek philosophy the word "despot" and its derivatives, first to designate authority within the household, and then to characterize a political system: when the legal tradition is neglected, when the subjects are enslaved, government degenerates and becomes despotic. Why was it that the word was not rediscovered in Venice until the sixteenth century—and then as the deformation *dispotico*—and why did it not gain currency until the seventeenth? If Aristotle was so familiar, what was being done with his terminology?

It was being preserved, disguised behind other words. During the Middle Ages, the Latin writings accepted only one borrowing from the Greek, the word *tyrannus*, and they shunned "despot," which then was translated either as *tyrannus* or as *dominus*.[179] In the thirteenth century, however, with William of Moerbeke's translations, *despoticus, despotica, despoticum*, and *despotizare* ultimately found their way into the Latin versions of Aristotle, and the words appear again in the writings of Thomas Aquinas, Marsilius of Padua, and William of Occam. The word made further headway in the fourteenth century when the Dominican Giordano introduced it into Italian. "Erode," he writes, "il quale dispoticamente governava [That which is governed despotically is undermined]." Nicolas Oresme, who translated Aristotle into French, appended to the text and commentary a definition of the despotic prince as a ruler whose subjects are slaves who no longer even remember what freedom is. In a kind of glossary at the end of his text, he places the term with "les moz qui sont propres à cette science de politiques ou qui ne sont pas en commun parler [words belonging to political science or that are not in common parlance]" and specifies that the meaning of the word is very close to that of tyranny: "Despotism is rule or lordship over serfs. And if they are justifiably serfs, such a prince is just. And if they are in servitude unjustly, through violence or fraud, that prince is despotic, oligarchical, tyrannical, or the like."[180]

A word that belongs to the jargon of political science, "despot" was not "common parlance." Along with its derivatives, it met with steady resistance in Latin as well as in French and in Italian. The humanists actually tried to keep it out of the political lexicon altogether. Arbiters of the classical language, they stopped its career, and in translations of Aristotle, *dominus, domestica,* and *dominatio* came to replace *despoticum, despotica, despoteia,* while in French, the words *seigneur* and *empire seigneurial* played that role. Loys Le Roy uses the latter terms in a new translation of Aristotle's *Politics,* to which he adds this commentary: "Such as the barbarian kingdoms, some of which, although legitimate and hereditary, still hold seignorial dominion [*empire seigneurial*], like the state of the Turk, of the Muscovite, and of the Preteian."[181] "Empire seigneurial," says Le Roy: this is in the year 1568, which is to say, after the writing of the *Methodus* and before the publication of the *République,* in which Bodin again employs the concept of "seignorial monarchy." Like Le Roy, Bodin considers it a legitimate monarchy—one that has been achieved through just war, is based on the rights of conquest, and is hereditary—and he does not confuse it with tyrannical monarchy, a degenerate and abusive form.

England aligned itself with continental positions. The 1598 translation of Aristotle, based on that of Le Roy, translates *empire seigneurial* as "maisterlike sway." In Knolles's 1606 translation of Bodin, *monarchie seigneuriale* becomes "lordly monarchy." It is only with Hobbes's *The Elements of Law, Natural and Politic* in the 1640s and *The Leviathan* in 1651 that the words "despotic" and "despoticall" finally enter the discourse of politics. But according to R. Koebner, to whom we owe a very fine analysis of the gradual rediscovery of the Aristotelian vocabulary in Europe, "despoticall," which signified lord, *seigneur,* or master, described the master's authority over his slave and was the opposite of "commonwealth" in the same way that government based on conquest is the opposite of government based on institutions. "Despoticall," then, did not have pejorative connotations (unlike "tyrannical"), and in the mid-seventeenth century, English readers were more familiar with the words "absolute" and "arbitrary" in connection with royal power than they were with the Greek adjective.[182]

To come back to France, the first occurrences of the word *despotique* which Koebner finds are in political texts from the Fronde, beginning in 1649. Pamphlets condemning the monarchy's unlimited power and the usurpation of that power by Cardinal Mazarin eventually began to make use of the Greek term, the translations of Aristotle's categories having lost their polemical impact. Even so, the term "tyrannical" was still the term most commonly used. In what is perhaps a sign of a lingering reluctance to speak Greek, the orthography of the word was still uncertain. In the famous pamphlet of 1652, *Les veritables maximes du gouvernement de la France*, of direct concern to us because of its reference to the Grand Signor, we read the following: "Les monarchies ne sont pas toutes d'Espotiques, il n'y que celle du Turc [Monarchies are not all despotic, only that of the Turk]."[183]

Though still exotic, the adjective nonetheless continued its French career. We should be grateful to Koebner for having traced these occurrences on both sides of the English Channel and for having found them in texts associated with political action as well as in philosophical texts. Koebner also underscores the near synonymy of "tyrannical" and "despotic" such as we have seen in the Venetian reports. But let us now return to Italy to refine the chronology he proposes.[184] At the time of the consolidation of the great absolutist states, Giovanni Botero, the anti-Machiavelli, made an important contribution to the theory of government with his *Della ragion di stato* (1583) and with two other works that are of particular concern to us here: *Le Relationi universali*, which he first began publishing in 1591 and which he continued to work on for the rest of his life, and *Il Discorso della legua contro il Turco*, published in 1614. In this later work, Botero demonstrated that the formation of a league was made impossible by the conflicting interests of the Christian princes. That idea, it turns out, was fairly commonplace, and the *Discorso* is not directly concerned with the nature of the Ottoman government. Far more remarkable is Botero's analysis of that government in the *Relationi*. There he defends the excellence of monarchy, even as he acknowledges that because all forms of government, whether simple or composite, have come into being in space and time, they are all capable of producing happiness or unhappiness. Nevertheless, he says, monarchy is built on the heavenly model and is therefore the preferable form. And the Turkish regime, which is of that form, is "very despotic." Let us listen to what he says:

Il governo de gli Ottomani è affatto despotico; perche il Gran Turco è in tal modo padrone d'ogni cosa compresa entro il confini del suo dominio, che gli habitanti si chiamano suoi schiavi, non che sudditi; e niune è padrone di se stesso, non che della casa, ove egli habita, o del terreno, ch'egli cultiva, eccetto alcune casate, che furono premiate, e privilegiate da Maometto II in Constantinopoli; e non è nissuno personnagio cosi grande, che sia sicuro della vita sua, non che dello stato, nel quale egli si trova, se no per la gratia del Gran Signore. Egli poi si mantiene in questo dominio, cosi assoluto con due mezi, cioè co'l torre affatto l'arme a' sudditi, e co'l metter ogni cosa in mano di rinegati, tolti per via di decima da gli stati suoi nella loro fanciullezza.[185]

[*The government of the Ottomans is completely despotic: for the Grand Turk is so much the master of all things contained within the bounds of his dominions, that the inhabitants account themselves his slaves, not his subjects; no man is master of himself, or of the house in which he lives, or of the fields he tills, except certain families of Constantinople whom Mohamet II has chosen and privileged; and there is no personnage so great that he stands secure in his life or in*

*his estate unless it so pleases the Grand Signor. He maintains such
absolute power in two ways: by disarming his subjects and by turning
everything over to the Renegados, whom he has taken in their
childhood as tithes from his states.*]

Note one further detail: in the 1617 French translation of this
text, the first sentence is rendered as follows: "Le gouvernement
des Ottomans est absolu, pour ce que le Grand turc est tellement
maistre de tout ce qui se trouve dans ses Estats, que les habitants
se nomment ses esclaves . . . [The government of the Ottomans
is absolute, for the Grand Turk is so much the master of everything in his states that the inhabitants are called his slaves]."[186] A
few lines down, *dominio cosi assoluto* becomes "cette seigneurie
absolue," further proof that the word "despotic" was not yet
established usage in France at the beginning of the seventeenth
century.

It was, however, in Venice. The point is not that the Venetian
ambassadors simply borrowed Botero's vocabulary: the diffu-
sion of Aristotelian terminology in Italy needs further investiga-
tion. We cannot ignore, however, the convergence of three series of events: changes in the political climate in Istanbul and in
Venice, struggles in the civic and religious arenas, and changes
in vocabulary. All these developments together are at play in the
variations of the Venetian discourse about the Porte, in the iden-
tification of the Ottoman regime with a tyrannical and then with
a despotic government, and finally in the proclamation of a di-
vorce between government based on violence against the governed and those forms of power that are based on law.

Finale

"From the end of the seventeenth century and throughout the eighteenth, a specter haunted Europe: the specter of despotism." With those words Alain Grosrichard in 1979 begins *Structure du sérail: La fiction du despotisme asiatique dans l'Occident classique*.[187] We have heard those words, or something like them, before; like a phrase from a fugue, they take up a familiar theme. Change a word or two, change the dates, and it is another specter that looms in the European imagination. But if we listen closely to what Grosrichard says, we can hear other variations developing. He offers a brilliant analysis of Montesquieu's formulations of the components and mechanisms of oriental despotism. Through readings of *Les lettres persanes* and *L'esprit des lois*, Grosrichard mines the documentary strata of travel accounts and descriptions of the Ottoman Empire in the latter half of the seventeenth century. Montesquieu had indeed read Baudier, Chardin, Ricaut, Tavernier; he had their works in his library, and from them he gathered the elements that allowed him to construct his category of despotism.[188] Grosrichard does not seek the empirical foundations of Montesquieu's theoretical discourse, its "true" material, in these textual strata of the age of classicism. For him, oriental despotism is "the concept of a fantasy,"[189] the fantasy of pure power. His task is therefore to trace its genealogy, to reveal its anatomy.

Grosrichard's superb demonstration raises a number of other questions that we are now in a position to answer. When was it that the specter of the despot emerged? In the eighteenth century? At the end of the seventeenth? With the Venetian reports, deeper strata open up. Standing at the crossroads of political action and political philosophy, the Serenissima's ambassadors provide a dual testimony—on the Ottoman Empire and on changes in the European political consciousness. For another specter had fallen across Europe, the specter of the tyrant. It had haunted European political thought since the Middle Ages, but its incarnation was believed to have been left behind in antiquity. Now it made its appearance among the crowned heads of the sixteenth century and began to drag its menacing shadow everywhere. As seen from Venice, the Ottoman emperor deprived his subjects of their freedom and had absolute power over them. Yet it was not until the final third of the sixteenth century that he was considered a tyrant. If the principles on which his power was based were at variance with those of the Venetian republic, the empire was nonetheless a construction of imposing beauty, an admirable order.

Toward the end of the sixteenth century and the beginning of the seventeenth, Europe completed its reinvention of Aristotle amid the tumult of political and religious battles. The word "despot" finally entered the lexicon of political thought. And now, to the opposition between despotic government and freedom was added another opposition, one that Aristotle had already established: the separation of Asia (or the Orient) from Europe. The distinctions between the various concepts designating particular forms of power and of state management were refined. The more definite the possibility of strong monarchies became, the more important it became to keep a distance from its extreme modalities. The specter had to be banished.

With regard to the Ottoman Empire, the moment of its slackening expansion, of its mounting difficulties, was not an imaginary one. But from the perspective of the Venetian observers, the properties characteristic of tyrannical and then despotic government took on particular relief: the use of fear as a principle of government; the paradox of the prince's absolute authority ceded to the grand vizier; the paradox of the vizier, whose life is always in jeopardy nonetheless; the monarch a prisoner in his own seraglio, growing soft and weak; the generalized corruption; the moral and spiritual debasement of the subjects. These leitmotifs that constitute despotism in Montesquieu were voiced by the Venetian ambassadors and repeated ad nauseam a good century before *L'esprit des lois*.

The ambassadors, and Montesquieu after them, clothed a Greek concept in the costume of the Grand Turk. But the monster, in truth, has not left us. The fantasy of pure power haunts us still; it continues to multiply in various guises. One is never done with the killing of Holofernes, for there are always other trappings for him to wear. ⌐

Acknowledgments

Now that this libretto is finished, I would so have liked to present it to Fernand Braudel. During his frequent visits to the *Annales*, I proposed a number of projects to him which he generally greeted with bemused skepticism. My Ottoman despot had the good fortune to intrigue him, and he referred me to a number of sources which were useful to me.

I also thank Danièle Kormos, the friend from my past whom I was fortunate to find again, for her translation—in the French edition of this book—of the citation in the Overture. Finally, my thanks go to Patricia Brown, Peter Brown, Philippe Buc, Michael Cook, Halil Inalcik, Charles Issawi, Cemal Kafadar, Krzysztof Pomian, Aline Rousselle, Eleanor Selfridge-Field, Randolf Starn, Lawrence Stone, the members of the 1987 Davis Center seminar at Princeton University, the members of my 1986 seminar at the Ecole des Hautes Etudes en Sciences Sociales, and Avram Udovitch for the suggestions they gave me at various moments in the preparation of this manuscript.

L. V.

Notes

Overture

1. "Relationi di Pietro Foscarini," in Nicolò Barozzi and Guglielmo Berchet, eds., *Le relazioni degli stati europei lette al Senato dagli ambasciatori veneziani nel secolo decimosettimo*, 5th ser.: *Turchia* (Venice, 1866), pt. 2: 89–90.

2. Ibid., 73, 77. My emphasis.

3. On the history of the word and the concept, see R. Koebner, "Despot and Despotism: Vicissitudes of a Political Term," *Journal of the Warburg and Courtauld Institutes* 14 (1951): 275–302; Franco Venturi, "Despotismo orientale," *Rivista Storica Italiana*, an. 72, fasc. 1 (1960): 117–126; Alain Grosrichard, *Structure du sérail: La fiction du despotisme asiatique dans l'Orient classique* (Paris, 1979).

4. François Quesnay, *Despotisme de la Chine* (1767), in *Oeuvres économiques et philosophiques de F. Quesnay, fondateur du système physiocratique* (Frankfurt and Paris, 1888), 563–660.

5. The expression was invented in the nineteenth century by German historians. Albert Soboul, *La civilisation et la Révolution française* 1 (Paris, 1970); Pierre Chaunu, *La civilisation de l'Europe des Lumières* (Paris, 1971). At the end of the seventeenth century, travelers to Russia such as Jean Chappe found the people there "apathetic" and "denatured" by despotism.

6. Nicolas-Antoine Boulanger, *Recherches sur l'origine du despotisme oriental* (1761), in *Oeuvres* (Amsterdam, 1794), 3:11–12.

7. Ibid., 15.

8. Venturi, "Despotismo orientale," 124ff.; Abraham Anquetil-Duperron, *Législation orientale, ouvrage dans lequel, en montrant quels sont en Turquie, en Perse et dans l'Indoustan les principes fondamentaux du Gouvernement, on prouve: (I) que la manière dont jusqu'ici on a représenté le Despotisme, qui passe pour être absolu dans ces trois Estats, ne peut qu'en donner une*

idée absolument fausse; (II) qu'en Turquie, en Perse et dans l'Indoustan il y a un Code de Lois écrites qui oblige le Prince aussi que ses sujets; (III) que dans ces trois Estats les particuliers ont des propriétés en biens meubles et immeubles dont ils jouissent librement (Amsterdam, 1778).

9. On Venetian diplomacy and ambassadorial reports, see Armand Baschet, *La diplomatie vénitienne: Les princes de l'Europe au XVIIe siècle d'après les rapports des ambassadeurs vénitiens* (Paris, 1862). The entire series of reports from the sixteenth century are found in Eugenio Albèri, *Relazioni degli ambasciatori veneziani al Senato durante il secolo decimosesto.* The reports from Istanbul appear in 3d ser., 1 (Florence, 1840), 2 (1844), 3 (1855), app. (1863). Seventeenth-century reports are in Barozzi and Berchet, *Relazioni.* Some of these reports have been reproduced in facsimile in Luigi Firpo, *Relazioni di ambasciatori veneti al Senato* vol. 13: *Costantinopoli, 1590–1793* (Turin, 1984). Included in this volume but not in Albèri's collection is a report by Leonardo Donà, presented in 1596 (309–370). As Albèri's edition does not follow chronological order, I list the reports in chronological order below and indicate by volume and page number where they appear in his collection. Further references to these reports mention only author and date:

Andrea Gritti (1503), 3:1
Antonio Giustiniani (1514), 3:45
Alvise Mocenigo (1518), 3:53
Bartolomeo Contarini (1519), 3:56
Marco Minio (1522), 3:69
Pietro Zen (1524), 3:93
Pietro Bragadin (1526), 3:99
Marco Minio (1527), 3:113
Pietro Zen (1530), 3:119
Daniello De Ludovisi (1534), 1:1
Bernardo Navagero (1553), 1:33
Anonymous (1553), 1:193
Domenico Trevisano (1554), 1:111
Antonio Erizzo (1557), 3:123
Antonio Barbarigo (1558), 3:145
Marino Cavalli (1560), 1:271
Andrea Dandolo (1562), 3: 161
Marcantonio Donini (1562), 3:173
Daniele Barbarigo (1564), 2:1
Luigi Bonrizzo (1565), 2:161

Jacopo Ragazzoni (1571), 2:77
Marcantonio Barbaro (1573), 1:299; appendix 387
Andrea Badoaro (1573), 1:347
Costantino Garzoni (1573), 1:369
Vicenzo Alesandri (1574), 2:103
Anonymous (1575), 2:309
Antonio Tiepolo (1576), 2:129
Giacomo Soranzo (1576), 2:193
Maffeo Venier (1579 or 1582), 1:437
Jacopo Soranzo (1581), 2:209
Anonymous (1582), 2:109 and 251
Paolo Contarini (1583), 3:209
Gianfrancesco Morosini (1585), 3:251
Maffeo Venier (1586), 2:295
Giovanni Michiel (1587), 2:255
Giovanni Moro (1590), 3:323
Lorenzo Bernardo (1592), 2:321
Matteo Zane (1594), 3:381
    10. Simon Contarini, in Barozzi and Berchet, *Relazioni.*

Part One

Judith

    11. Angelo Ventura, "Scrittori politici et scritture di governo," in *Storia della cultura veneta, a cura di G. Arnaldi* (henceforth abbreviated as *SCV*) 3, pt. 3 (Vicenza, 1981): 513–563.

    12. Margaret L. King, *Venetian Humanism in an Age of Patrician Dominance* (Princeton, 1986); Angelo Ventura, *Relazioni degli ambascaiatori veneti al senato* (Bari, 1976), xix.

    13. Andrea Palladio, *The Four Books of Architecture* (New York, 1965), bk. 1, chap. 1: 1.

    14. Oliver Logan, *Culture and Society in Venice, 1470–1790: The Renaissance and Its Heritage* (London and New York, 1972).

    15. Paolo Preto, "I Turchi et la cultura veneziana del seicento," in *SCV* 4, pt. 2 (1984): 313–341.

    16. Baschet, *Diplomatie vénitienne*, 26; Ventura, *Relazioni degli ambascaiatori veneti*, introduction.

    17. Philippe Braunstein and Robert Delort, *Venise, portrait historique*

d'une cité (Paris, 1971), 131ff.; Francesco Gaeta, "L'idea di Venezia," in *SCV* 3, pt. 3: 565–641, and "Venezia da 'Stato misto' ad aristocrazia 'esemplare,'" in *SCV* 4, pt. 2: 436–494; King, *Venetian Humanism*, xviii; Ventura, *Relazioni degli ambascaiatori veneti*, xliii.

18. On the political dimension of public rituals, see Edwin Muir, *Civic Ritual in Renaissance Venice* (Princeton, 1981).

19. Baschet, *Diplomatie vénitienne*, 51.

20. Ibid., 54ff. Ventura, *Relazioni degli ambascaiatori veneti*, ci. Baschet seems to have been unaware of the French editions of *Le trésor politique*, for he does not include them in his inventory.

21. Marcel Bataillon, "Mythe et connaissance de la Turquie en Occident au milieu du XVIe siècle," in *Venezia e l'Oriente fra tardo medievo e rinascimento, a cura di Agostino Pertusi* (Venice, 1966), 451–470; Giuliano Lucchetta, "L'Oriente mediterraneo nella cultura di Venezia tra quattro e cinquecento," in *SCV* 3, pt. 2 (1980): 375–432.

22. On the report as a codification of Venetian political discourse, see Piero Del Negro, "Forme e istituzioni del discorso politico veneziano," in *SCV* 4, pt. 2: 407–436; Ventura, "Scrittori politici."

23. Baschet, *Diplomatie vénitienne*, 26; Ventura, "Scrittori politici."

24. Preto, "I Turchi et la cultura veneziana," 324; Federico Seneca, *Il doge Leonardo Donà* (Padua, 1959).

25. Simon Contarini, in Barozzi and Berchet, *Relazioni*, 127.

26. Ventura, "Scrittori politici," 557.

27. Fernand Braudel, *The Mediterranean and the Mediterranean World in the Age of Philip II*, trans. Siân Reynolds (New York, 1973); Braunstein and Delort, *Venise, portrait historique*; Michel Lesure, "Notes et documents sur les relations vénéto-ottomanes, 1570–1573," *Turcica* 4 (1972): 134–164, and 8, no. 1 (1976):117–156; Paolo Preto, *Venezia e i Turchi* (Florence, 1975), chap. 2: 25ff., in particular.

28. A. da Mosto, *I dogi di Venezia nella vita publica e privata* (Milan, 1960), 235–246, on Gritti. See also Lucchetta, "Oriente mediterraneo."

29. According to da Mosto, the biographer of Georgio Gritti calls him Pietro. Ibid., 243. Nothing is known of Gritti's third son.

30. Ibid. On Alvise, see Benedetto Ramberti, *Delle cose de' Turchi* (Venice, 1539).

31. Fernand Braudel, "Bilan d'une bataille," in *Il Mediterraneo nella seconda metà del '500 alla luce di Lepanto, a cura di Gino Benzoni* (Florence, 1974), 109–120; Preto, *Venezia e i Turchi*, 210–214, reports that Alvise had converted to Islam.

32. On *Juditha*, listen to the work itself. Berlin Chamber Orchestra, Vittorio Negri, dir. (Philips, 1974); or more recently, National Orchestra of Hungary, Ferenc Dzekeres, dir. (Compact-disc Hungaroton, 1986). See also Denis Arnold and Elsie Arnold, *The Oratorio in Venice* (London: Royal Musical Association monographs 2, 1986); Lino Bianchi, *Carissimi Stradella: Scarlatti e l'oratorio musicale* (Rome, 1969); Eleanor Selfridge-Field, "*Juditha* in Historical Perspective: Scarlatti, Gasparini, Marcello, and Vivaldi," in *Vivaldi, Veneziano Europeo, a cura di Francesco Delgrada* (Florence, 1980), 135–153; Eleanor Selfridge-Field, "Music at the Pietà before Vivaldi," *Early Music* 14 (1986): 373–386. Judith is also the subject of an epic poem in six cantos by Marko Marulić, composed and published in Venice in 1521 in the same patriotic and anti-Turkish key.

Holofernes

33. Navagero (1553), 65.
34. Barbaro (1573), 315.
35. Gritti (1503), 18.
36. Minio (1522), 71; Zen (1524), 95; Barbarigo (1564), 3.
37. Anonymous (probably 1582), 439.
38. Barbaro (1573), 302.
39. De Ludovisi (1534), 4; Contarini (1583), 216.
40. Garzoni (1573), 428. Also Navagero (1553) 35; Barbarigo (1564), 3.
41. Erizzo (1557), 127. As late as 1583, Paolo Contarini, not wanting to burden his report with details of which, he says, the books are full, "simply" observes "that a large part of Africa, most of Europe, and a very large part of Asia have now submitted to this empire."
42. Barbarigo (1564), 5ff.
43. Garzoni (1573), 371.
44. Minio (1522), 71.
45. Ibid., 72.
46. Badoaro (1573), 357.
47. Tiepolo (1576), 133.
48. Garzoni (1573), 425.
49. A *timar* was a district entrusted to a cavalryman, or *timariote*; its revenues permitted him to raise and arm troops in times of war and to see to his own needs in times of peace.

50. Cavalli (1560), 280; Barbarigo (1564), 33ff.
51. Garzoni (1573), 390.
52. Barbaro (1573), 309, 313; Tiepolo (1576), 135. For the perspectives of recent historiography on this subject, see p. 79.
53. Garzoni (1573), 411; Tiepolo (1576), 146, notes, however, the lack of oarsmen in the navy.
54. Garzoni (1573), 419.
55. Dandolo (1562), 166.
56. Minio (1522), 75.
57. Cavalli (1560), 280; Barbarigo (1564), 33.
58. Barbaro (1573), 301.
59. Tiepolo (1576), 170.

In the Heart of the Seraglio

60. Contarini (1583), 216. Note the late date of this assessment.
61. Navagero (1553), 95ff. See also Badoaro (1573), 356ff.; Garzoni (1573), 377ff.
62. Morosini (1585), 265.
63. Badoaro (1573), 356ff., and especially Garzoni (1573), 377ff.
64. Navagero (1553), 65.
65. De Ludovisi (1534), 6.
66. Barbaro (1573), 328.
67. De Ludovisi (1534), 6.
68. Barbaro (1573), 326ff.
69. Trevisano (1554), 147–148.
70. Erizzo (1557), 134.
71. Erizzo (1557) 131; Barbaro (1573), 327–328; Garzoni (1573), 432; Moro (1590), 343; Bernardo (1592), 33.
72. Minio (1522), 73; Erizzo (1557), 131; Barbarigo (1558), 149; Barbarigo (1564), 33.
73. Minio (1522), 73; De Ludovisi (1534), 6; Erizzo (1557), 131; Barbarigo (1558), 149; Barbarigo (1564), 33.
74. Gritti (1503), 27–28, 38–39.
75. Giustiniani (1514), 48; Mocenigo (1518), 53, 59; Minio (1527); Navagero (1553), 72.
76. Tiepolo (1576), 166.
77. Mocenigo (1518), 59.
78. Donini (1562), 176.

79. On the coincidence of political and religious values in Venice, see King, *Venetian Humanism*, 106.

80. Minio (1522), 74; Barbarigo (1558), 148; Dandolo (1562), 164.

81. Contarini (1519), 58; Giustiniani (1514), 50.

82. Garzoni (1573), 403.

83. Ibid.

84. Gritti (1503), 19; Navagero (1553), 56, 79; Erizzo (1557), 133; Cavalli (1560), 281.

85. Erizzo (1557), 138.

86. Garzoni (1573), 401–402; Barbaro (1573), 321.

87. See the brilliant article by Roberto Zapperi, "Arrigo le velu, Pietro le fou, Amon le nain et autres bêtes: Autour d'un tableau d'Agostino Carrache," *Annales, ESC*, no. 2 (March-April 1985), 307–327.

88. Romano Canosa, *Storia dell'Inquisizione in Italia dalla metà del cinquecinto alla fine del settecento*, vol. 2: *Venezia* (Rome, 1987), 136–139.

89. Gritti (1503); Erizzo (1557), 137; Barbarigo (1558), 160; Barbaro (1573), 317.

90. Erizzo (1557), 136.

91. Paul Veyne, *Bread and Circuses: Historical Sociology and Political Pluralism*, trans. Brian Pearce (London, 1990), 14. The reality of the situation is obviously more subtle than what the ambassadors say. In the Ottoman Empire, too, according to the rules of the political game if not in its actual practice, corruption is condemned. And in Venice, in spite of the myth in which members of the patriciate took comfort, some of them did, on occasion, turn to shady practices. See Donald E. Queller, *The Venetian Patriciate: Reality versus Myth* (Urbana, Ill., 1986).

The Prophecy of Daniel

92. Erizzo (1557), 139.

93. Navagero (1553), 35; Contarini (1583), 217.

94. Morosini (1585), 256–257.

95. Contarini (1583), 217.

96. Mocenigo (1518), 53.

97. Barbarigo (1558), 148.

98. Navagero (1553), 37; Barbaro (1573), 305.

99. Barbaro (1573), 301–302.

100. Badoaro (1573), 351; Contarini (1583), 217; Moro (1590), 333.

101. Robert Folz, *L'idée d'Empire en Occident du Ve au XIVe siècle* (Paris, 1953), 1l82. On later echoes of "imperial messianism" in the sixteenth century, see Jean Delumeau, *La civilisation de la Renaissance* (Paris, 1967).

102. G. Gracco, "La cultura giuridico-politica nella Venezia della 'serrata,'" in *SCV* 2 (1976): 238–271.

103. Jacques Le Goff, *La civilisation du Moyen Age* (Paris, 1964), 183ff.

104. J. H. Franklin, *Jean Bodin and the Sixteenth-Century Revolution in the Methodology of Law and History* (New York, 1963), 117 n4.

105. F. E. Manuel, *Shapes of Philosophical History* (Stanford, Calif., 1965), 14.

106. Ibid., 18.

107. D. Cantimori, *Eretici italiani del cinquecento* (Florence, 1939), 14–16. In the pamphletary literature and news sheets of the day, these prophecies translate into the repeated announcements of disasters in Istanbul and the conversion of the sultan to the true faith.

108. Giovanni Tarcagnota, *Delle istorie del mondo* (Venice, [1585] 1588); Agostino Ferentilli, *Discorso universale* (Venice, 1570).

109. Guillaume Postel, *De la république des Turcs* (Poitiers, 1560). See Frank Lestringant, "Guillaume Postel et l'obsession turque," *Actes du Colloque Guillaume Postel, Avranches, 1981* (Paris, 1985).

110. Barbaro (1573), 301; Barnardo (1592), 401. As late as the beginning of the seventeenth century, Ottaviano Bon considers that the empire lacks good principles of government which otherwise "would open for it the way to monarchy" (1608), 117; Simon Contarini (1612), 152–153, in Barozzi and Berchet, pt. 1.

111. Gritti (1503), 18; also Badoaro (1573), 351; Moro (1590), 333.

112. Donà (1596), 299–301, in Firpo.

113. Sanuto, *Diarii*, 46: 132–133. On the prophecy of the conquest of Rome which was circulating in Istanbul, see Ragazzoni (1571), 84–85, which reports the vizier's words.

114. Much more could be said about the imperial ideology and the staging of power at the Sublime Porte. I confine myself here to what the Venetian ambassadors say about it and how they perceive it. See Gülru Neciboglu, "The Formation of an Imperial Tradition: The Topkapi Palace in the 15th and 16th Centuries" (Ph.D. diss., Harvard University, 1986), and Halil Inalcik, "State and Ideology under Sultan Suleyman I," in H. Inalcik, *The Middle East and the Balkans under the Ottoman Empire* (Bloomington: Indiana University Turkish Studies and Turkish Ministry of Culture Joint Series, vol. 9, 1993), pp. 70–94.

Chorus

115. The word *ordine* occurs frequently in Trevisano (1554); the words *bellissimo, dilettevole, meraviglioso, superbissimo,* in Garzoni (1573); all of them in Badoaro (1573), etc.

116. Erizzo (1557), 139.

117. Preto, *Venezia e i Turchi,* 495; Preto, in *SCV* 4, pt. 2: 314, in particular.

118. About a thousand publications on the Ottoman Empire between 1501 and 1550 have been counted, and for the second half of the sixteenth century the number is about 2500, according to Carl Gölner, *Turcica: Die Europäischen turkendrücke des XVI Jahrhunderts,* 2 vols. (Bucharest and Berlin, 1961–1968), cited in C. J. Heywood, "Sir Paul Rycaud, a Seventeenth-Century Observer of the Ottoman State: Notes for a Study," in E. K. Shaw and C. J. Heywood, *English and Continental Views of the Ottoman Empire, 1500–1800* (Los Angeles, 1972), 31–59.

119. We should stress that, despite their limitations, these orderings are extremely valuable and make it possible to steer through a scholarly production of great density. For France, see Geoffroy Atkinson, *Les nouveaux horizons de la Renaissance française* (Paris, 1935); C. D. Rouillard, *The Turk in French History, Thought, and Literature* (Paris, 1941). For Venice, see Preto, *Venezia e i Turchi;* Stéphane Yerasimos, "De la collection de voyages à l'histoire universelle: La 'Historia universale de Turchi' de Francesco Sansovino," in a forthcoming issue of *Turcica.* From a broader perspective, but for an earlier period, R. Schwoebel, *The Shadow of the Crescent: The Renaissance Image of the Turk (1453–1517)* (Nieuwkoop, 1967).

120. Perry Anderson, *Lineages of the Absolutist State,* 2d ed. (London, 1975), 462.

121. Ibid.; also Preto, *Venezia e i Turchi,* who refers to the same passage.

122. Nicolo Machiavelli, *"The Prince" and Other Political Writings,* trans. Bruce Penman (London, 1982), 53.

123. Nicolo Machiavelli, *The Discourses,* book 1, chap. 19, trans. Christian E. Detmold, in *"The Prince" and "The Discourses"* (New York, 1950), 173.

124. Ibid., 192.

125. Ibid., introduction to book 2: 273.

126. Anderson, *Lineages of the Absolutist State,* 398. See also Lawrence

Krader, *The Asiatic Mode of Production: Sources, Development, and Critique in the Writings of Karl Marx* (Assen, 1975), 21–22 n1. Krader situates Bodin among the ancestors of the notion of Asiatic despotism while emphasizing that the Turks are put not into the category of tyranny but into that of seignorial monarchy.

127. Jean Bodin, *Method for the Easy Comprehension of History*, trans. Beatrice Reynolds (New York, 1945). [Some of the translations of quotations from the *Methodus* which appear in this text follow the French translation by Pierre Mesnard, *La méthode de l'histoire* (Algiers, 1941). In those cases, I cite the page in the French version first, followed by the corresponding page number of the English version in brackets—*Tr.*]

128. Bodin read other works as well on the Turks. See Reynolds, trans., *Method for the Easy Comprehension of History*, 378.

129. *La méthode de l'histoire*, 165 [179].

130. Ibid., 193 [204].

131. Reynolds, trans., *Method for the Easy Comprehension of History*, 272.

132. *La méthode de l'histoire*, 289–290 [292–293].

133. Jean Bodin, *Les six livres de la République*, 6 vols. (Paris, 1986) [Published in English as Jean Bodin, *The Six Bookes of a Commonweale*, a facsimile reprint of the English translation of 1606, corrected and supplemented in the light of a new comparison with the French and Latin texts, ed. Kenneth Douglas McRae (Cambridge, 1962)—*Tr.*]. The other occurrences of the Turk in *The Six Books* point in the same direction: they illustrate practices that have positive connotations. For example, in book 1, the Turks are spoken of as almost the only people in the world for whom nobility is measured by virtue, not by ancestry; in book 4, Bodin mentions the prohibition against bearing arms in peacetime, which helps prevent sedition. At no time is the empire spoken of as a tyranny.

134. Etienne de La Boétie, *Le discours de la servitude volontaire*, ed. P. Léonard (Paris, 1976), 135; translated by Malcolm Smith, under the title *Slaves by Choice* (Egham Hill, Surrey, England, 1988), 54.

135. Ibid., 127 [50, in translation].

Part Two

"Greater tyranny the world has never seen"

136. [The title quotation is from Morosini, 1585.—*Tr.*] This second series of reports includes the following: Tiepolo (1576); Venier (1579 or 1582 [uncertain attribution]); an anonymous report (1582); Soranzo

(1581); Contarini (1583); Morosini (1585); Venier (1586); Moro (1590); Bernardo (1592); Zane (1594); Dona (1596); Nani (1600 and 1603); the famous description of the seraglio by Ottavio Bon; and finally, reports by Contarini (1612) and Valier (1616). In content and expression, some of the reports from the first series, Barbaro's in particular, are transitional to the second. See p. 94 and p. 94 n162.

137. Contarini (1612), 154; Bernardo (1592), 350; Nani (1600), 32. On the changes in the rhetoric of the sixteenth-century ambassadors, see Piero Del Negro, "Forme a istituzioni del discorso politico veneziano," in *SCV* 4, pt. 2: 435–436.

138. Bernardo (1592), 321–426.

139. Contarini (1583).

140. Tiepolo (1576), 183–185; Moro (1590), 325; Venier (1579 or 1582), 460.

141. Especially Bernardo (1592), 334, 359, 360.

142. Morosini (1585), 285ff. In describing the empire, however, he is unstinting with his superlatives. Venier (1586) 297–298.

143. Venier (1579 or 1582), 460, 467–468; Morosini (1585), 282.

144. Morosini (1585), 269.

145. Anonymous (1582), 229; Morosini (1585), 282.

146. Venier (1579 or 1582), 439; Morosini (1585), 273; Moro (1590), 326.

147. Morosini (1585), 284; Moro (1590), 330.

148. Bernardo (1592), 326, 398.

149. Morosini (1585), 267.

150. Bernardo (1592), 398.

151. Morosini (1585), 255; Zane (1594), 386.

152. Donà (1596), 358.

153. Nani (1603), 35.

154. Montesquieu, *L'esprit des lois*, bk. 13, chap. 13.

155. Nani (1603), 35; Venier (1579 or 1582), 441; Moro (1590), 337.

156. Bernardo (1592), 381.

157. Ibid., 326, 364, 398; Moro (1590), 329.

158. Moro (1590), 328; Bernardo (1592), 364, 373, and later reports.

159. Venier (1579 or 1582), 439–440.

160. Bernardo (1592), 351.

161. Morosini (1585), 279.

162. Navagero (1553), 40–41. Cavalli (1560) speaks of the Pasha. Barbaro (1573), 307. Note two exceptions in the series that follows: neither Soranzo nor Valier uses the notion of tyranny.

163. This series includes reports by Cappello (1634), Contarini (1636 and 1641), Foscarini (1637 and 1641), Quirini (1676), Morosini (1680), Civrano (1682), Donado (1684).

164. Valier (1616), 278.

165. Venier (1579 or 1582), 439. Prior to this date, "despot" is a title; it is used to designate the sultan's vassal princes in Moldavia, Croatia, and so forth.

At the Sublime Porte

166. Stanford J. Shaw, *History of the Ottoman Empire and Modern Turkey*, (Cambridge, 1976), 1: 169ff., summarizes all the arguments based on "conventional" historiography. See also V. J. Parry in M. A. Cook, ed., *A History of the Ottoman Empire to 1730* (Cambridge, 1976), chap. 4: 103–132.

167. Ilkay Sunar analyzes the integrative role of the political center in "Anthropologie politique et économique de l'Empire ottoman et de sa transformation," *Annales, ESC*, nos. 3–4 (May-August 1980), 551–579.

168. Halil Inalcik, *The Ottoman Empire: The Classical Age, 1300–1600*, trans. Norman Itzkowitz and Colin Imber (London, 1973), chap. 4: "The Decline of the Ottoman Empire," 41–52.

169. On classical imperial ideology, see Inalcik, "State and Ideology under Sultan Suleyman I." The realization of the empire's malaise is the subject of a pioneering article by Bernard Lewis, "Ottoman Observers of Ottoman Decline," *Islamic Studies* 1 (1962): 71–87. See also Cornell Fleischer, "Royal Authority, Dynastic Cyclism, and 'Ibn Khaldunism' in Sixteenth Century Ottoman Letters," *Journal of Asian and African Studies* 18 (1984): 218–237; Cemal Kafadar, "When Coins Turned into Drops of Dew and Bankers Became Robbers of Shadows: The Boundaries of Ottoman Economic Imagination at the End of the Sixteenth Century" (diss., McGill University, 1986).

170. Kafadar, "When Coins Turned into Drops of Dew"; Andreas Tietze, ed. and trans., *Mustafā Ālî's Counsel for Sultans of 1581* (Vienna, 1979).

171. Andreas Tietze, "The Poet as Critic of Society: A Sixteenth-century Ottoman Poem," *Turcica* 9, no. 1 (1977): 120–160, which deals with Mustafa Ali. For the case of the *cadi* Veysi, see Lewis, "Ottoman Observers of Ottoman Decline," 74–78.

172. *Venezia e la difesa del Levante da Lepanto a Candia, 1570–1670*, catalogue from the exhibition at the Arsenale in Venice (1986).

173. Venier (1586), 305.

174. Robert Mantran, "L'Impero ottomano, Venezia, e la guerra (1570–1670)," in *Venezia e la difesa del Levante*, 227–232.

The Abduction from the Seraglio

175. See William J. Bouwsma's classic work *Venice and the Defense of the Republican Liberty: Renaissance Values in the Age of the Counter Reformation* (Berkeley, Calif., 1968; 2d ed., 1984); Preto, "I Turchi et la cultura veneziana," 313–341.

176. On Florence, see Albèri, *Relazioni*, 2d ser., vol. 1: 325, 327; vol. 2: 76–78, 371.

177. Barozzi and Berchet, *Relazioni*, 4th ser: *Inghilterra* (Venice, 1863).

178. Michel Lesure, "Les relations franco-ottomanes à l'épreuve des guerres de religion (1560–1594)," in Hâmit Batu and J.-L. Bacqué-Grammont, eds., *L'Empire ottoman, la République de Turquie, et la France*, Varia Turcica 3 (Istanbul-Paris, 1986), 37–57. Lesure cites the pamphlet, also mentioned in Rouillard, *The Turk in French History*, 414, titled *La France-Turquie, c'est-à-dire conseils et moyens tenus par les ennemis de la couronne de France pour réduire le royaume en tel estat que la tyrannie turquesque* [France-Turkey; or, Counsels and means of the enemies of the crown of France to reduce the kingdom to a state like that of Turkish tyranny—*Tr.*] (Orleans, 1576). Pierre Mesnard, *L'essor de la philosophie politique au XVIᵉ siècle*, 2d ed. (Paris, 1977), in a note on page 321, quotes Théodore de Bèze: "Tel Empire (celui des Turcs) ne se doit point appeler Roial ni humain, mais entièrement barbare, tyrannique, bestial et abominable" [Such an empire (that of the Turks) ought to be called neither royal nor human, but completely barbarous, tyrannical, bestial, and abominable]," *Du droit des magistrats sur leurs sujets* (1575), 92. For the empire, see Kenneth Setton, "Lutheranism and the Turkish Peril," *Balkan Studies* 3 (1962): 133–139.

179. See the fine study by Koebner, "Despot and Despotism."

180. "Despotie est princey ou seigneurie sur serfz. Et se ilz sont iustement serfz tel prince est iuste. Et se ilz sont en servitude iniustement par violence ou par fraude ce est princey despotique, olygarchique, tyrannique ou semblable."

181. *Les politiques d'Aristote esquelles est monstree la science de gouverner le genre humain en toutes especes d'estats publiques*, par Loys le Roy, dict

Regius, de Costentin (Paris, 1568), 373; cited in Koebner, "Despot and Despotism," 284.

182. Two other indications: Francis Bacon, in *The Essayes or Counsels, Civill and Morall*, written between 1597 and 1625, uses the term "tyranny" in speaking of the Turks: "A Monarchy, where there is no Nobility at all, is ever a pure, and absolute tyranny; As that of the Turkes" (ed. M. Kiernan, Oxford, 1985, 41); Knolles, *Generalle Historie of the Turkes*, 1603, titles his second chapter "Absoluteness of the Emperor," but in Savage's abridged 1704 edition of Knolles, the title becomes "Le pouvoir *despotique* du sultan" (my emphasis).

183. In the same year as this pamphlet, *La Mercuriale* proclaims: "Si le souverain exerce un empire despotique sur les sujets, il n'est plus Roy, mais tyran, parce que l'empire légitime qu'il a sur eux est politique et non despotique [If the sovereign rules his subjects despotically, he is no longer a king but a tyrant, because legitimately, his dominion over them is political and not despotic]." Cited by Charles Jouhaud, *Mazarinades: La Fronde et les mots* (Paris, 1985), 157.

184. Koebner, "Despot and Despotism," 288ff., credits Hobbes with having added the words "despotic" and "despoticall" to the stock of terms used in political discourse in Europe. This chronology should be corrected, at least for Italy.

185. Giovanni Botero, *Relationi universali*, pt. 2, bk. 4: 1st ed. (Venice, 1591). I have consulted the editions of 1599 and 1640.

186. This (loose) French translation of Botero's book, *Les estats empires et principautez du Monde . . .* , is by Pierre Davity (Paris, 1617), 1275.

Finale

187. Alain Grosrichard, *Structure du sérail: La fiction du despotisme asiatique dans l'Occident classique* (Paris, 1979).

188. Muriel Dodds, *Les récits de voyages, sources de "L'esprit des lois" de Montesquieu* (Paris, 1929).

189. "Le concept d'un fantasme" is the title of the second chapter of this fine work.

Index

Library of Congress Cataloging-in-Publication Data

Valensi, Lucette.
    [Venise et la Sublime Porte. English]
    The birth of the despot : Venice and the Sublime Porte / Lucette
Valensi ; translated by Arthur Denner.
        p. cm.
    Includes bibliographical references and index.
    ISBN 0-8014-2480-1
    1. Turkey—Foreign public opinion, Venetian. 2. Public opinion—
Italy—Venice. 3. Turkey—History—1453-1683. 4. Despotism.
5. Europe—Intellectual life—Turkish influences. I. Title.
DR479.I8V3513 1993
949.61'015—dc20   93-1352

www.ingramcontent.com/pod-product-compliance
Lightning Source LLC
Chambersburg PA
CBHW030654270326
41929CB00007B/365